HANDY REFERENCE

To go to a Web page:
Enter the URL in the Address bar, then p...

If you change your mind:
Abort the download by clicking Stop.

To record the location of a page:
Select Add to Favorites from the Favorites menu.

To return to that page:
Select it from the Favorites menu.

Keyboard shortcuts:
Ctrl+O .... Open page or file
F5 .... Reload current page
Esc .... Stop loading

Alt+Cursor Left .... Go back
Alt+Cursor Right .... Go forwards
Page Down .... Scroll down page
Page Up .... Scroll up page
Home .... Go to beginning of page
End .... Go to end of page

Ctrl+F .... Find text
Ctrl+A .... Select all the text
Ctrl+C .... Copy selected text
Ctrl+V .... Paste selected text

Ctrl+P .... Print page or frame

Internet Mail and News shortcuts:
Ctrl+N .... New message
Ctrl+R .... Reply to author
Ctrl+G .... Reply to newsgroup
Ctrl+F .... Forward message
Delete .... Delete message

ABOUT THE SERIES

In easy steps series is developed for time-sensitive people who want results fast. It is designed for quick, easy and effortless learning.

By using the best authors in the field, and with our experience in writing computer training materials, this series is ideal for today's computer users. It explains the essentials simply, concisely and clearly - without the unnecessary verbal blurb. We strive to ensure that each book is technically superior, effective for easy learning and offers the best value.

Learn the essentials **in easy steps** - accept no substitutes!

Titles in the series include:

Title	Author	ISBN
Windows 95	Harshad Kotecha	1-874029-28-8
Microsoft Office	Stephen Copestake	1-874029-37-7
Internet UK	Andy Holyer	1-874029-31-8
CompuServe UK	John Clare	1-874029-33-4
CorelDRAW	Stephen Copestake	1-874029-32-6
PageMaker	Scott Basham	1-874029-35-0
Quicken UK	John Sumner	1-874029-30-X
Microsoft Works	Stephen Copestake	1-874029-41-5
Word	Scott Basham	1-874029-39-3
Excel	Pamela Roach	1-874029-40-7
Sage Sterling for Windows	Ralf Kirchmayr	1-874029-43-1
Sage Instant Accounting	Ralf Kirchmayr	1-874029-44-X
SmartSuite	Stephen Copestake	1-874029-42-3
HTML	Andy Holyer	1-874029-46-6
Netscape Navigator	Mary Lojkine	1-874029-47-4
PagePlus	Richard Hunt	1-874029-49-0
Publisher	Brian Austin	1-874029-56-3
Access	Stephen Copestake	1-874029-57-1
Internet Explorer	Mary Lojkine	1-874029-58-X
WordPerfect	Stephen Copestake	1-874029-59-8

To order or for details on forthcoming titles ask your bookseller or contact Computer Step on 01926 817999.

INTERNET EXPLORER
in easy steps

Mary Lojkine

In easy steps is an imprint of Computer Step
5c Southfield Road, Southam
Warwickshire CV33 OJH England
☎01926 817999

First published 1996
Copyright © 1996 by Computer Step

Notice of Liability
Every effort has been made to ensure that this book contains accurate
and current information. However, Computer Step and the author
shall not be liable for any loss or damage suffered by readers as a
result of any information contained herein.

Trademarks
Microsoft, Windows and ActiveX are registered trademarks of
Microsoft Corporation. All other trademarks are acknowledged as
belonging to their respective companies.

For all sales and volume discounts please contact Computer Step on
Tel: 01926 817999.

For export orders and reprint/translation rights write to the address
above or Fax: (+44) 1926 817005.

Comments to the publisher can be e-mailed to:
harshad@compstep.demon.co.uk

Printed and bound in the United Kingdom

ISBN 1-874029-58-X

Contents

CHAPTER ONE

Getting Started

Before you can make use of Internet Explorer, you need to know a bit about the Internet. This chapter provides a brief introduction, then explains how to obtain, install, configure and run Internet Explorer.

Covers

Introduction to the Internet

The Internet is a 'network of networks' which connects millions of computers from all around the world. It's estimated that more than 40 million people have access to the Internet, and this number increases every day.

You can use the Internet to access general and specialist news services, research anything from aardvarks to zwitterions and find out more about your favourite sport, hobby, television programme or pop group. You can also send messages to people all around the world, participate in discussion groups and obtain software for your computer.

History of the Internet

The Internet has its roots in 1969, when the US Government decided to connect some of its computers so scientists and military agencies could communicate more easily. Because the Cold War dominated American politics at the time, the system was designed to withstand a nuclear attack. There was no central control centre; each machine operated independently and messages travelled from one computer to another by whatever route seemed most convenient.

In the 1970s several more computer networks were established by military and academic institutions. Eventually many of these networks were linked together, creating the network of networks we now know as 'the Internet'. Throughout the 1980s the Internet was dominated by scientists, academics, computer experts and students, but in the 1990s it has become accessible to a much wider range of people.

No one owns or controls the Internet and the infrastructure is somewhat shambolic. It can be creaky, cranky and intensely irritating, but for the most part everything works very well. You can connect to a computer in New York just as easily – and as cheaply – as to one in York, England. Although some parts of the world are better represented than others, the Internet is becoming a truly global phenomenon.

The World Wide Web

The recent surge of media interest in the Internet is mostly due to the World Wide Web. Developed in 1990 at CERN, the European Laboratory for Particle Physics, the Web consists of millions of magazine-style pages containing text and images, plus multimedia elements such as sound samples, animations and video clips.

'Browsing' the Web is a lot like using a multimedia CD-ROM, but the material you're looking at could come from anywhere on the Internet. The pages are connected together by hypertext links, enabling you to move about by clicking on underlined text or highlighted images. You can also go directly to a particular page if you know its address.

For more about Slate, Microsoft's on-line magazine, see page 65.

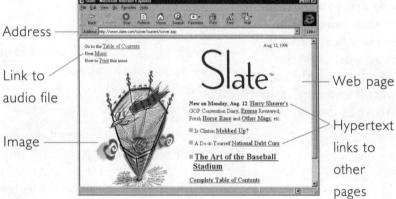

Address

Link to audio file

Image

Web page

Hypertext links to other pages

Web Browsers

In order to look at – or 'browse' – Web pages, you need a piece of software called a Web 'browser'. It enables you to find Web pages and display them on your screen.

Microsoft's Web browser program is called Internet Explorer. It has quite a bit in common with Explorer, the file management utility provided with Windows, and is very easy to use. It's also free, making it the ideal choice if you're on a budget.

1. Getting Started **9**

Connecting to the Internet

Before you can access the Web, you need to be connected to the Internet. There are three possibilities: your company or university may provide a direct connection; you can visit a cyber café; or you can use a modem (a device which enables computers to communicate with each other over a phone line) to connect your home computer to the Internet.

Company Connections

The rest of this chapter assumes you're using a dial-up connection (see opposite). If you are connecting from a university or company, you'll need your system manager's help to install and configure Internet Explorer.

If you work for a university, or a large company which has an internal computer network, you may already be connected to the Internet. Buy your systems manager a drink and ask if it's possible for you to access the World Wide Web from your PC, Macintosh or workstation. He or she may be horrified by the prospect, but with a bit of luck you'll soon be exploring the Web.

The advantage of a company connection is that you don't have to pay for it. There are two disadvantages: you have to be at work to access the Internet, and you have no control over the speed of the connection, which can be anything from excellent to awful.

Cyber Cafés

The cyber café is the Internet equivalent of the public telephone, but generally warmer and more comfortable. You can drink coffee (or beer, in a cyber pub) and use the café's computers to explore the Internet. There are over 50 cyber cafés in the UK, with more opening every month.

Charges vary, but you can expect to pay around £2.50 for half an hour on the Internet. Some cafés also operate a membership system, enabling you to have your own e-mail address and send and receive messages.

If you aren't sure whether the Internet is for you, visiting a cyber café is a good way to get a feel for the services it offers. You don't have to worry about obtaining or installing software, and there's generally someone to help with any problems. You are, however, stuck with whatever software the café provides, and you can't set things up to suit your particular needs.

...contd

Dial-up Connections

The most versatile option is to use a modem to connect your own computer to the Internet. Regrettably, this is also the option which requires the most input – both financial and technical – from you.

You need five things to establish a dial-up connection:

1 A computer. Internet Explorer is available for both PCs and Apple Macintoshes, but this book concentrates on the Windows version for PCs.

2 A modem. Modems come in two flavours – internal and external – and a range of speeds. It's a false economy to buy anything less than a 28,000bps (bits per second) modem; a slower modem may be cheaper, but you'll run up bigger phone bills. Consult your favourite computer magazine for more information and reviews.

HANDY TIP

You won't be able to receive phone calls while you're 'on-line' (connected to the Internet), so you may want to invest in an answering service, such as BT's Call Minder.

3 A telephone line. If your phone company offers cheap deals on local calls, so much the better.

4 An Internet service provider (see page 12). A service provider has a computer system which is permanently connected to the Internet, and to a bank of modems. You use your modem to connect to one of the service provider's modems, via your telephone line, thereby making your computer (temporarily) part of the Internet.

5 Connection software. You'll need a TCP/IP utility to establish the connection (see page 13).

Internet Service Providers

Service providers enable you to connect to the Internet. Most also provide basic Internet software and help you set it up. There are two types of provider:

Unless your telephone line is supplied by a cable company which offers free local calls, you'll also be running up your phone bill while you're connected to the Internet.

1 Regular service providers, such as Demon Internet and Direct Connection, simply enable you to connect to the Internet. They generally charge a flat monthly fee, no matter how much (or how little) time you spend on-line.

2 On-line services, such as the Microsoft Network (MSN) and CompuServe, provide additional facilities for their members, such as private discussion forums. They have traditionally been more expensive than regular service providers, but there isn't much difference now.

The best way to find a provider is by word of mouth. If you don't have any friends on the Internet, see what people are saying in the letters pages of Internet magazines.

Most Internet magazines publish up-to-date lists of Internet service providers. The things to consider when choosing a provider are:

1 Level of service. Make sure you'll be getting full Internet access, including e-mail, newsgroups and the Web. Your provider must also support the PPP connection protocol – you won't be able to use Internet Explorer if it doesn't.

2 Points of Presence (PoPs). Try to find a service provider which has an access point within your local call area, otherwise your phone bill will be astronomical.

3 Subscriber-to-modem ratio. If your service provider has lots of subscribers and hardly any modems, you'll find it difficult to get through. A ratio of 30:1 is passable, 15:1 is good.

4 Technical support. Call up and ask a few questions. If you can't understand the answers, try another provider.

Connection Software

You need special software to access the Internet – an ordinary comms package won't do.

Before you can run Internet Explorer, or any other Internet application, you need to be able to persuade your modem to connect your computer to the Internet. You do this with a small program called a winsock, which dials your modem and establishes a TCP/IP interface, enabling other programs to send and receive data. TCP/IP stands for Transmission Control Protocol/Internet Protocol, but fortunately you don't ever need to know anything about it – your winsock takes care of all the technical bits.

Internet Explorer requires a 32-bit winsock, such as the one built in to Windows 95. You can't use it with a 16-bit winsock.

Windows 95 has a built-in winsock. It's normally quite difficult to configure, but Internet Explorer includes an Internet Setup Wizard which makes things much easier.

Once the winsock is configured correctly, you can use it to dial in to your service provider's computer, or 'log on'. Depending on your setup, it may transmit your user name and password automatically, or require you to enter them manually. You leave the winsock program running in the background while you use Internet Explorer.

Broadly speaking, 'log on' means to make a connection. As well as logging on to the Internet, you can log on to particular services. Conversely, 'log off' means to disconnect.

When you've finished browsing the Web, you end your session by clicking the Disconnect button. This tells your modem to hang up, releasing the phone line for other calls. Most setups will drop the line if the modem is inactive for a long time (20-30 minutes), but it's better for your phone bill if you remember to hang up straight away.

Obtaining Internet Software

REMEMBER

'Download' means to copy a file from a computer on the Internet to your computer. Uploading a file copies it from your computer to one on the Internet.

One of the many paradoxes of the Internet is that you can download all the software you need to get connected – except that you can't, because you need to be connected before you can download anything.

Consequently, most service providers supply some start-up software, which may include a copy of Internet Explorer. Alternatively, Microsoft's Internet Starter Kit – available from High Street stores – includes a copy, and Internet Explorer sometimes appears on the CD-ROMs attached to many popular computer magazines. If you've only just bought your PC, you may even find that Internet Explorer has been pre-installed.

If you're already an Internet user, you can download Internet Explorer from Microsoft's Web site – see opposite for instructions. You may also find that your service provider makes it available via a local FTP site or bulletin board. If you're technically inclined, this is often a better solution, because downloading Internet Explorer from a relatively quiet local site will almost certainly be quicker than fetching it from one of Microsoft's servers.

Once you're connected to the Internet, you can obtain any other software you require from Web sites or one of the many vast FTP archives – see Chapter Eleven.

Downloading Internet Explorer

If you're currently using some other Web browser, you can download Internet Explorer from Microsoft's Web site.

1 Connect to the Internet Explorer Home Page at:
`http://www.microsoft.com/ie/`

2 This page changes regularly, but it's always linked to the download area. Look for a 'Download' or 'Download Area' button or some underlined text which says something like 'Download Internet Explorer' or 'Get it now'. Click on the button or the text to move to the download page.

It takes at least 20-30 minutes to download Internet Explorer, so it's best to fetch it while the Internet is fairly quiet. Mornings are usually better than evenings, because most Americans are still in bed.

3 The download page also changes regularly. Read the instructions, then select the appropriate version and click the Download button to copy the file on to your hard disk. You may be presented with a list of locations which you can download the software from; choose one which is reasonably close to home. You're also likely to be asked which folder you want it saved into – if you have a temp folder, that will do nicely.

4 Follow the instructions overleaf to install Internet Explorer.

Essential Information

HANDY TIP

If your copy of Internet Explorer was supplied by your service provider, it may have been config- ured for you, in which case you'll be able to skip most of the next five pages.

REMEMBER

Every computer on the Internet has an IP address – a set of four numbers which uniquely identifies it. Some service providers give each member a personal IP address, but most just 'lend' you any available address each time you log on. DNS servers convert word-based addresses such as www.microsoft.com **into numerical IP addresses. See page 26 for more about Internet addresses.**

As discussed previously (see pages 11 and 12), you'll need to set up your modem and open an account with an Internet service provider before you can access the World Wide Web, or any other Internet service. You then need to gather together the following information about your account so that you can install and configure Internet Explorer:

1 Name of service provider.

2 User name and password.

3 The phone number you dial to connect to the Internet.

4 Your IP address and subnet mask (only required if your service provider uses static IP addresses – most don't).

5 Domain Name System (DNS) server address(es).

6 Whether or not you'll be logging on via a terminal window (unless your service provider tells you otherwise, assume that you will be).

Most of these details should be on the information sheets sent by your service provider when you opened the account – if there's anything you can't find, give your service provider a ring.

While you're collecting information, it's a good idea to note down your e-mail address and the names of your provider's mail and news servers. You're likely to need these details later on.

Installing Internet Explorer

If you're installing Internet Explorer from disks supplied by your service provider, follow whatever instructions have been provided. They should include details of any service-specific settings or options. Likewise, if you've bought the Internet Starter Kit, follow the on-screen instructions.

If you're installing Internet Explorer from a magazine's cover-mounted CD-ROM, you probably just have to pick the right menu option. Check the magazine's disc pages if you have any problems.

Finally, if you've downloaded Internet Explorer from Microsoft's Web site, you'll have ended up with a file called something like msie30.exe. It's a self-extracting archive – a compressed file which contains everything you need to install and run Internet Explorer. To install the program itself, you must:

 This book generally assumes that you'll use Explorer to locate files rather than clicking on the My Computer icon. You'll find Explorer in the Programs section of the Start menu.

1 Double-click on the My Computer icon and locate this file. Alternatively, use Explorer (the Windows file management utility) or the Find command to track it down.

2 Double-click on the icon filename. Once the components have been extracted, the setup program runs automatically.

Some versions of the installation routine ask you which folder Internet Explorer should be installed into; others use a preset folder. Likewise, some versions run the Internet Setup Wizard (see overleaf) automatically, while others don't activate it until you try to run Internet Explorer. All versions add a new icon, called The Internet, to your Windows desktop.

The Internet

The Internet Setup Wizard

REMEMBER

These instructions should work for most people with standard dial-up accounts. If you have problems, it may be that your computer setup or account requires you to make slightly different choices. Contact your service provider for more specific advice. Note also that your version of the Internet Setup Wizard may be slightly different from the one shown here, and you will need to enter the details of your account, rather than the example values shown here.

The Internet Setup Wizard enables you to configure the built-in winsock by answering a few simple questions and entering the details of your Internet account.

If the Wizard didn't run automatically at the end of the Internet Explorer installation process, double-click 'The Internet' icon on your desktop to start it. After each step below, click on Next.

I There are three setup options. Automatic is for people who don't yet have Internet accounts. It connects you to Microsoft's referral service so that you can choose a local

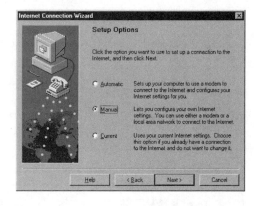

service provider. Internet Explorer will then be configured automatically. Choose Manual if you've opened an account, but haven't started using it yet, or Current if your computer is already set up for Internet access. The rest of these instructions are for people who've chosen the Manual setup option.

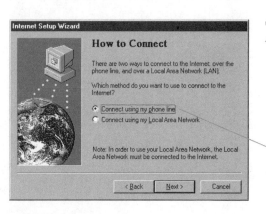

2 Unless you're connecting via a company network – see page 10 – select Connect using my phone line.

3 Microsoft's Internet Mail utility (see Chapter Twelve), is easier to use than Windows Messaging, so you'll probably want to select No.

4 The Wizard may then ask you for your Windows CD-ROM and install some files.

5 Enter the name of your service provider.

6 Enter the phone number you use to connect to the Internet. Unless your provider says otherwise, leave the Bring up terminal window... box checked.

7 Enter your user name and password.

8 If your service provider has given you a personal IP address, enter it. Otherwise, select the first option: My Internet Service Provider...

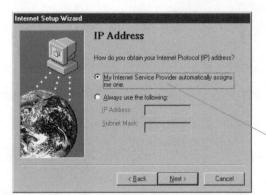

HANDY TIP

If you need to run the Wizard again, perhaps to update your details, go to the Start menu and select Programs>Accessories>Internet Tools>Get on the Internet.

9 Enter the address(es) of your service provider's DNS server(s). You may then be asked to restart your computer.

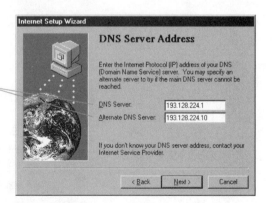

You're now ready to run Internet Explorer, connect to the Internet and start exploring the Web. You'll also be able to run other Internet software, such as e-mail and news-reading programs (see Chapters Twelve and Thirteen).

Running Internet Explorer

If you want to connect to the Internet without running Internet Explorer, go to the Programs section of the Start menu, select Accessories and click on Dial-up Networking. This will bring up a folder containing an icon for your service provider; double-click on it to bring up the Connect To dialogue box.

To run Internet Explorer, simply double-click on its icon. You'll find it on your desktop, and in the Programs section of your Start menu, either in the main listing or under Accessories (in an Internet Tools folder).

The Internet

When you double-click on the icon, Internet Explorer runs the built-in winsock program (see page 13), enabling you to establish a connection to the Internet.

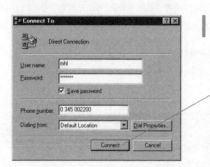

I Click Connect to dial into your service provider's computer (see page 11) and connect to the Internet.

Assuming you've left the Bring up terminal window... box checked (see page 19), the next thing you see is the Post-Dial Terminal Screen.

When you establish a connection, a modem icon 🔲 **appears at the right-hand end of your Task bar. Its lights flash green when you are downloading data.**

2 The contents of this screen vary from service to service. Follow your provider's log-on procedure, then click Continue or press F7.

You are automatically taken to Microsoft's Web site, where you can register your browser. Chapter Two explains how to move about this site and visit other places on the Web.

3 To end your session, switch to the Connected To dialogue box and click the Disconnect button.

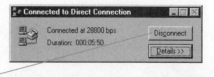

Upgrading to the Latest Version

If you've installed an older version of Internet Explorer, you'll probably want to upgrade to the latest release as soon as you've mastered the basics (see Chapter Two). You can download the upgrade from Microsoft's Web site.

1 Connect to the Internet Explorer Home Page at:
`http://www.microsoft.com/ie/`

HANDY TIP

You might also want to get some of the add-ons for Internet Explorer. Once you've found the download area, look for an 'extra components' or 'additional features' link.

2 This page changes regularly, but it's always linked to the download area. Look for a 'Download' button or some underlined text which says 'Download Internet Explorer' or 'Get it now', and click on it.

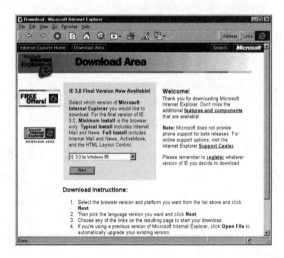

3 Read the instructions, then select the latest version and click Next or Download. You will probably be offered a selection of download sites.

4 When you see this dialogue box, click Open it to upgrade your version automatically, or Save it to disk to copy it into a folder on your hard disk. If you choose the latter, you'll need to locate and run the

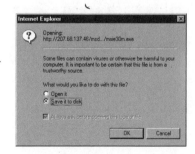

downloaded file (see page 17) once you've logged off.

CHAPTER TWO

Basic Web Browsing

Internet Explorer enables you to locate and view Web pages. This chapter gets you started.

Covers

Areas of the Screen

Like most Windows programs, Internet Explorer has title, menu and tool bars across the top of the window, and a status bar at the bottom. The most important areas of the screen are:

Title bar –
displays the
name of
the page

Menu bar

Button bar

Address bar –
displays the address,
or URL, of the page

Explorer logo –
animated if the
program is busy

Links bar – click
here to replace
the Address bar
with icons for
five of your
favourite
Web sites

Status bar

Main window, where
Web pages are displayed

The Button, Address and Links bars are collectively referred to as the 'Toolbar'. The icons on the Button and Links bars change colour when the mouse pointer is over them, indicating that you're in the right place for a particular function. If you hold the mouse pointer over one of the icons for a second or two, a yellow label pops up and tells you what it does.

Customising the Screen

You can enlarge the main window by rearranging the Button, Address and Links bars, or by turning them off altogether. You can also turn off the Status bar.

You can replace the Microsoft sites on the Links bar with five of your own favourite sites – see page 50.

1 To expand the Links section, grab its 'handle' (the two vertical lines at the left-hand end) with the mouse. Hold down the left mouse button and drag the bar downwards.

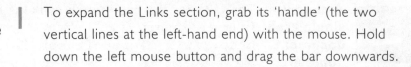

The three sections can be arranged in many different ways – just keep dragging the handles until you find a layout which works for you.

2 To compress all three sections into a single bar, drag the Address and Links sections to the right-hand end of the Button bar. Click on Address or Links when you want to access either of these sections.

3 To compress the bar even further, hold the mouse over the divider at the top of the main window until it turns into a two-headed $\updownarrow$ arrow, then drag the divider upwards.

To turn off individual bars, select Options from the View menu and go to the Toolbars section of the General page.

4 To turn off all three bars, pull down the View menu and uncheck Toolbar. You can also turn off the Status bar, but you'll miss out on a lot of useful information if you do. To reinstate either item, pull down the View menu and reselect it.

Understanding URLs

Every page on the Web has a unique address. These addresses are called Uniform Resource Locators, or URLs. You've probably already seen some URLs on television.

 REMEMBER

A page is a single Web document. Some are quite long – use the scroll bar to move through them. You can also press Home and End to move to the top and bottom of the page.
A site is a collection of related pages, and the server is the computer on which all the documents are stored.

The URL for the page which explains how to personalise Internet Explorer is:

`http://www.microsoft.com/ie/ie3/personal.htm`

The 'http:' indicates that this is a Web page.

This is the name of the server where the page is stored.

This section tells your browser which directory the page is stored in.

This is the name of the document which describes the page.

Web pages' URLs always begin with http: (it stands for HyperText Transfer Protocol). You may also come across URLs for other types of Internet site:

URL Begins	Type of Site	See Chapter
ftp:	FTP	Eleven
gopher:	Gopher	Eleven
mailto:	E-mail address	Twelve
news:	Usenet newsgroup	Thirteen

Abbreviated URLs

URLs for major sites are generally quite short. The URL for the Internet Movie Database (see page 74) is:

http://uk.imdb.com/

If the URL doesn't specify a particular document, Internet Explorer automatically looks for an index file. As long as the person in charge of the Web site has provided one, the first two parts of the address are enough to locate the site.

Entering a URL

If you know the address of the Web page you wish to visit, you can simply enter it into Internet Explorer. There are two ways to do this:

 Sometimes it takes a while for Internet Explorer to download and display a page. Check the Status bar to find out what's happening, or look at the Explorer logo. If it's animated, Internet Explorer is still working. You can abort a download by clicking the Stop button or pressing the Esc key.

1 Type it into the Address bar, then press the Enter key. Internet Explorer will find the page and display it.

2 If you have turned off the Toolbar, you can enter URLs by selecting Open... from the File menu or pressing Ctrl+O. Both actions bring up the Open dialogue box. Enter the URL and click the OK button.

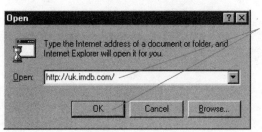

 Chapter Six contains some URLs for you to try. You'll also find lots of URLs in most Internet magazines.

You must get the URL absolutely right, otherwise Internet Explorer won't be able to locate the page. In particular, make sure the capitalisation is correct – you can't substitute an 'a' for an 'A' – and don't let any spaces creep in. URLs never contain spaces.

What If It Doesn't Work?

The Internet is constantly evolving: sites come and go and servers are constantly being moved or upgraded. It's also subject to its fair share of bugs and bad connections, so sometimes Internet Explorer will give you an error message instead of displaying the page you were looking for.

Three of the most common error messages are:

HANDY TIP

You can sometimes find a page which has moved by entering part of the URL. Start by leaving out everything after the last slash (/). If that doesn't work, keep chopping off sections until you get back to the name of the server (see page 26).

1 File Not Found. There are numerous variations on this message, but they all amount to one of two things: either you typed the URL incorrectly, or the page you were looking for has been moved or deleted.

HTTP/1.0 404 Object Not Found

The Internet Movie Database

Something wasn't found.

The URL you requested could not be found. The usual cause for this is an out of date link on another site.

Please try starting here instead.

2 Timed Out. This message appears because the computer you are trying to connect to is busy. These problems often clear themselves quite quickly, so try again in a minute or two.

3 No Connection. This message usually appears because you aren't connected to the Internet. Call up the Dial-Up Networking folder (see page 21) and double-click on your service provider's icon to establish a connection.

Using Links

If you could only get to Web pages by typing in their URLs, browsing the Web would be tedious and time-consuming. Fortunately there's a much easier way to get about: links.

Almost every Web page is linked to anything from one to a hundred or more other pages. Links are usually indicated by coloured, underlined text, and you move to the linked page by clicking on this text. For example:

Links can also take you to another section of the same page. For example, many long pages have a list of the major subheadings at the top. Clicking on one of the headings takes you straight to the relevant section.

1 Here's a page from the BBC's Web site (see page 75). If you click on the blue underlined text which says 'Films'...

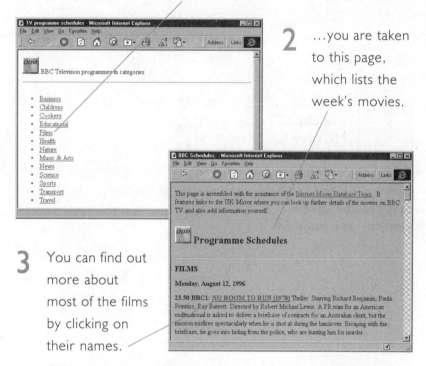

2 ...you are taken to this page, which lists the week's movies.

3 You can find out more about most of the films by clicking on their names.

You can tell when the mouse pointer is over a link, because it changes into a pointing hand. While you're pointing, check the Status bar: you should see the name of the file or site at the other end of the link. Note also that the text usually changes colour when you click on it, so that you can see where you've been.

Images can also be used as links – see page 35.

Retracing Your Steps

By now you'll have realised that browsing the Web is like exploring the back streets of an old market town – there are lots of directions to head in and it's easy to get lost. Fortunately, it's equally easy to retrace your steps.

1 To return to a page you visited recently, click on the Back button, select Back from the Go menu or press Alt+Cursor Left.

2 Once you've gone back a few pages, you may want to go forward again. Click on the Forward button, select Forward from the Go menu or press Alt+Cursor Right.

You can use the History folder to return to any page you've visited in the last two or three weeks – see page 54.

3 You can speed up the process using the Go menu, which lists the pages you've visited most recently (the current page – marked with a tick – is usually at the bottom). Select the page you want to return to.

4 If you get completely lost, you can return to your Start Page by clicking the Home button or selecting Start Page from the Go menu. (Your Start Page is the page Internet Explorer looks for each time you run it. It's usually a Microsoft page, but you can change it to anything you like – see page 51.)

Saving Web Pages

HANDY TIP

If you're only going to read a page once, there's no need to save it – just log off. The page will still be loaded and you can scroll through it as usual.

Sometimes you'll want to read a lengthy Web page at your leisure, without worrying about your phone bill, or to keep the information handy for reference. The easiest solution is to save it on to your hard disk. You can then reload it whenever you want, without connecting to the Internet.

1 To save a Web page, pull down the File menu and select Save As File… This brings up the standard Windows Save As dialogue box.

File	
New Window	Ctrl+N
Open...	Ctrl+O
Save	Ctrl+S
Save As File...	
New Message...	
Send To	▶
Page Setup...	
Print...	Ctrl+P
Create Shortcut	

2 Choose a folder and give the file a name, then click Save. Note that this only saves the text; if you also want the images, you have to save them separately – see page 37.

3 To reload a saved page, select Open from the same menu, or press Ctrl+O. Click the Browse button, locate the file and click Open.

4 Alternatively, use Explorer (the Windows file management utility) to locate the file and double-click on it. This option will also open Internet Explorer, if necessary.

Don't forget that text on the Web is protected by copyright. Keeping a copy of a Web page for personal reference is unlikely to get you into trouble, but you must not reuse or redistribute material without the author's permission.

Printing Web Pages

If you're gathering information for a report or project, printing Web pages is sometimes more convenient than saving them. Printing a page preserves the images as well as the text, without filling up your hard disk, and you can scribble notes in the margins or highlight important passages. You can also print a table showing all the Web pages linked to the current one.

1 To print the current page, pull down the File menu and select Print, or press Ctrl+P.

2 If you want to include a table of links at the end of the document, make sure the Print shortcuts... box is checked.

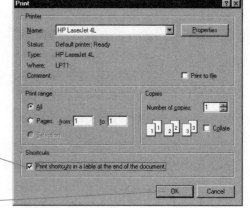

3 Click the OK button to print the page.

CHAPTER THREE

Images, Sound and Video

One of the things which makes the Web different from any other Internet service is its support for multimedia elements, including pictures, sounds and videos. This chapter explains how to make the most of them.

Covers

Viewing Images

Without support for images, the Web would never have captured the imagination of the general public. They make it colourful and interesting, add personality and give it the 'friendly face' which Windows users have come to expect. Some are merely decorative; others illustrate or amplify the text, and many are used as links (see opposite).

Internet Explorer usually loads the text for a page first, then the pictures. Image files are typically five to ten times larger than text files, and take proportionately longer to download, so at first you'll just see little placeholder graphics. Sometimes these have a word or two of 'alternative' text describing the image. Note that you don't have to wait for all the images to appear before you move on to another page – you can click on a link to another section of the site at any point.

If you see an icon with a red cross ⊠ where an image should be, Internet Explorer either can't find the image file, or can't display it. There's nothing you can do about this.

You'll notice that some images arrive line by line, while others start off blocky and gradually become more detailed. This is due to differences in the file format, rather than anything you can specify in Internet Explorer.

Interactive Images

Most Web images are static, just like the pictures in a book. However, you'll also come across some pages which use computer technology to add motion or change the pictures at regular intervals.

1 Animations: Some animated images are actually little video clips (see page 39), but most use a multiframe version of the popular GIF image format. Server-push and Java can also be used to create animations (see pages 101–2) .

2 Webcams: A Webcam displays frames 'sliced' out of live footage from a video camera. The image is updated regularly, giving you a minute-by-minute view of a fish tank, office, volcano eruption or space shuttle mission, to name a few of the most popular subjects.

Images as Links

Images can also be used to link pages together. The three most common types of image links are:

1   Buttons. Many Web sites, including NASA's shuttle pages (see page 82) use toolbar-style buttons to make it easy for you to find your way from page to page.

2   Text. When Web page designers want to use a special font, create fancy text effects or combine text with graphics, they have to save the result as an image file. For example, the menu shown below (from Microsoft's site – see page 64) is a set of images – one for each item. The menu text is neither blue nor underlined and hence doesn't appear to be linked, but clicking on an item still takes you to the appropriate section of the site.

3   Thumbnails. Clicking on a small picture often takes you to a larger version of the same image.

You can find out whether an image is a link by moving the mouse pointer over it. If it changes to a pointing hand, just as it does over a text link, clicking will take you to another page. Check the Status bar while the pointer is over the image to find out what's at the other end of the link.

Image Maps

Some images contain more than one link. For example, the opening image on the MGM/UA site (see page 74) looks like a regular picture, but each of the six film posters is linked directly to a page dealing with that particular film. It's essentially a visual menu.

This type of image is called an image map, because different sections of the picture are 'mapped' to different Web page addresses. Sometimes you can find out where each section will take you by looking at the Status line, but often you just have to click around and see what happens.

Saving Images

If you want to be able to view an image again – without having to connect to the Internet – save it on to your hard disk. You can then access it whenever you want, either by loading it back into Internet Explorer, or by opening it in an art package.

 Almost all the images on the Web are in JPG or GIF format. You can open both types of file with many art packages and most image conversion utilities.

Don't forget, though, that images on Web sites are subject to copyright, just like images in books. It's unlikely that anyone will object to you creating a private 'electronic scrapbook', but reusing an image elsewhere, especially for commercial purposes, is asking for trouble.

1 To save an image on to your hard disk, right-click on it and select Save Picture As... from the pop-up menu.

Open
Open in New Window
Save Target As...

Save Picture as...
Set as Wallpaper

Copy
Copy Shortcut

Add to Favorites...
Properties

2 This brings up the standard Save As dialogue box. Select a folder and check that the file has a meaningful name.

Save As

Save in: Pictures

hubble1.gif
hubble2.gif
mccmap.gif
shuttle.gif
newmcc.gif
shuttle launch.GIF

File name: moon

Save as type: GIF (*.gif)

Save
Cancel

3 Click the Save button to finish.

4 To reopen the image in Internet Explorer, select Open from the File menu or press Ctrl+0. Click Browse and locate the file, then click Open and OK to load it into the main window.

Wallpaper

Internet Explorer can also replace your current wallpaper with an image from the Internet.

HANDY TIP

The NSSDC site is located at:

`http://nssdc.gsfc.nasa.gov/`

1 When you've found a suitable image, such as this picture of the Earth from the National Space Science Data Centre's Web site, right-click on it and select Set As Wallpaper from the pop-up menu…

HANDY TIP

Some Web pages have a background image behind the text. To save it, right-click on the page and select Save Background As... or Set As Wallpaper from the pop-up menu.

2 …to transfer it directly to your desktop.

Large images work best, although you can always tile smaller ones – see Windows Help for details.

Playing Sounds and Videos

REMEMBER

You'll need a correctly configured soundcard to play sound files.

HANDY TIP

Internet Explorer supports most common sound formats, including Windows (wav), Macintosh (aiff), basic audio (au and snd), MIDI (mid) and MPEG audio. It can also play Video for Windows (avi), QuickTime (qt and mov) and MPEG movies.

Sound samples and video clips may seem as different as radio and television, but Internet Explorer treats them as much the same thing. Both can be either embedded in a Web page or linked to it, and they are downloaded, played and saved in exactly the same way.

Embedded sounds and videos are downloaded automatically when you open a Web page. Embedded sounds play in the background, providing an introductory fanfare or an accompanying melody, and embedded video clips are incorporated into the page. You don't have to do anything to activate an embedded file – they are played automatically. You can, however, halt the playback of a tune that's getting on your nerves by clicking the Stop button.

It's more common for sounds and videos to be linked to a page, so that you can decide whether or not you want to download them (sound files are generally larger than image files, and videos can be huge, so you'll want to avoid both if you have a slow modem). When you click on the link, the file is downloaded, usually into a separate window with tapedeck-style controls (see overleaf). You can then play it as many times as you want.

Sometimes the controls are incorporated into the page, as they are in this example from Microsoft's site. They work just the same way, though.

Playing a linked sound or video is a two-step process: first you download the file, then you play it.

1. To play a sound or video, such as these recordings from the NBA Web site (see page 78), click on the link to download the file.

AUDIO

■ **Game 4:** Michael Jordan says last season's semifinals loss to Orlando helped focus the team and himself. (**468k wav** | **RealAudio**)

■ **Game 4:** Jordan looks ahead to a possible Finals matchup with Seattle. (**679k wav** | **RealAudio**)

2. Internet Explorer automatically opens the player window. The blur line creeps across to the right, indicating the progress of the download.

3. Click the Play button ▶ to hear the sound or watch the video clip.

4. Click the Close button ☒ in the top right corner to finish.

Once the file has started downloading into the player window, you can switch to another Windows application and get on with something else, or go back to the main window and wander off round the Web. The sound or clip will continue downloading, even though you're no longer looking at the page it was linked to. However, your modem can only receive so much data at once. If you try to look at image-heavy pages at the same time as you're fetching a file, everything will get very, very slow.

Note also that you don't have to download the file completely; in many cases you can play the first few seconds as soon as the blue line has moved a few millimetres across the screen. It's a good idea to do this with large files, in case the rest isn't worth waiting for. Close the player window to abort a transfer.

RealAudio

RealAudio is a 'streaming' sound format; the files are transferred in real time. This means that you can listen to them as they are downloaded, rather than having to wait until some or all of the file has reached your computer.

RealAudio is used to 'Webcast' radio shows and news bulletins and provide live coverage of special events. It can also be used for recorded sound samples, giving you more or less instantaneous playback. Sound quality deteriorates when the Internet is very busy, but most of the time it's acceptable, especially for voice broadcasts.

You need a 14,400 or 28,800bps connection to listen to RealAudio (ra or ram) files, which are automatically transferred to the special RealAudio player.

1 Click on a link to download a RealAudio sound file.

AUDIO

■ **Game 4**: Michael Jordan says last season's semifinals loss to Orlando helped focus the team and himself. (**468k wav** | **RealAudio**)

2 The sample is transferred to the RealAudio player. It begins playing almost immediately.

■ **Game 4**: Jordan looks ahead to a possible Finals matchup with Seattle. (**679k wav** | **RealAudio**)

HANDY TIP

The RealAudio controls can also be embedded in a Web page using ActiveX technology – see Chapter Nine.

3 If you're listening to a live broadcast, you can leave the player running in the background while you carry on working in another application.

You can find out more about RealAudio from the Progressive Networks Web site – see page 83.

Saving Sounds and Videos

Saving sounds and videos is slightly different from saving images: you right-click on the link rather than on the file in the player.

1 Right-click on the link which leads to the sound or video and select Save Target As... from the pop-up menu.

2 This brings up the Standard Save As dialogue box. Check the file name and folder and click Save.

You don't have to listen to or view the file before you save it. However, you might as well: once you've downloaded and played a file, Internet Explorer saves it from memory rather than downloading it again.

You can play the saved file by loading it back into Internet Explorer or any other suitable sound or video utility.

1 To load a sound or video file, such as this clip from one of NASA's sites (see page 82), select Open from the File menu or press Ctrl+O. Select All Files from the Files of type: list and locate the file, then click Open and OK.

2 The sound or video is automatically transferred to the player window.

Turning Everything Off

The multimedia elements make the Web more fun to browse, but they can take a long time to download. If you have a slow modem, or are using the Web at a busy time, you may want to turn off the images, sounds and videos.

1 To turn off the multimedia elements, select Options… from the View menu and click on the General tab.

2 Uncheck the pictures, sounds and videos boxes.

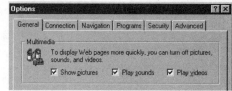

3 You will now see placeholder icons instead of pictures, and you won't hear or see embedded sounds and videos (linked sounds and videos still play normally).

Many sites use image maps and image-based toolbars to help you get about easily, so turning off the images can make it difficult to find your way from page to page. The embedded sounds and videos are generally no great loss, though.

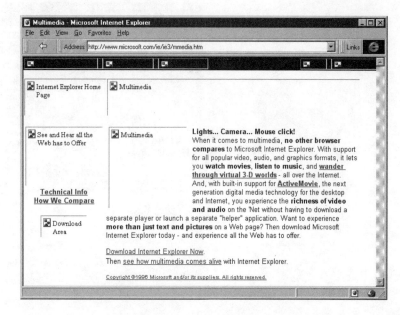

You can get the images back when you come to a particularly interesting page, or when you need them switched on to navigate.

1. To view an individual image, right-click on the placeholder icon and select Show Picture from the pop-up menu. —

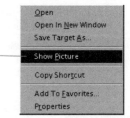

2. To view all the images on a page, go back to the Options dialogue box and reselect Show Pictures. Click the Refresh button, select Refresh from the Go menu or press F5 to reload the page.

3. The page is restored to its normal appearance.

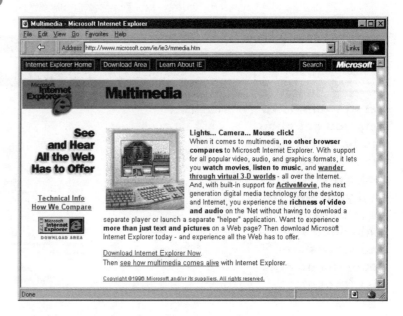

CHAPTER FOUR

Finding Your Way

There are well over 20 million Web pages and it's easy to lose your way as you jump from one to the next. This chapter explains how to use Favorites, Internet Shortcuts and the Links bar to keep track of the ones you find most useful or interesting. It also shows you how to make the most of the Start and Search pages.

Covers

Creating Favorites

As you explore the Web, you'll often come across sites which you may want to visit again in the future. Rather than writing down the URL, you can add the site to Internet Explorer's Favorites menu. This menu is like the Programs section of the Start menu – the only real difference is that selecting an item takes you to a Web site rather than running a program.

You can also create Favorites by right-clicking on the current page, or on a link. The latter action creates a Favorite for the page at the other end of the link.

1 To create a Favorite for the current page, select Add to Favorites... from the Favorites menu.

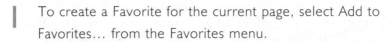

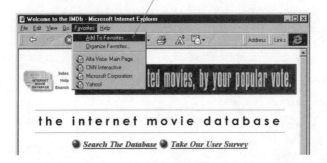

The default name for a Favorite is the title of the page, as displayed in Internet Explorer's title bar.

2 You may want to change the name to something shorter or clearer. Once you've done so, click OK.

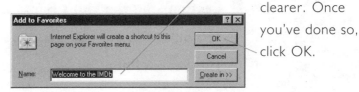

3 You can now return to this page any time you want, simply by selecting it from the Favorites menu.

You can also access the Favorites menu by clicking on the Favorites icon in the Button bar.

Organising Your Favorites

Favorites Folders
Once you have 15-20 Favorites, you'll want to start organising them into folders. This creates submenus and makes it easier to find the one you want.

1 Select Organize Favorites... from the Favorites menu.

2 Click the Create New Folder 🗂 button, then type in a name for your folder and press Return.

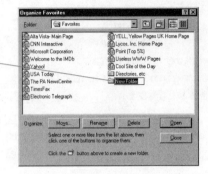

HANDY TIP **Once you've created one or more folders, you can save new Favorites directly into the correct folder – simply click the Create in>> button and select a folder before you click OK. You can also make a folder as you save a Favorite – click Create in>> , then click New Folder.**

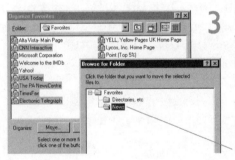

3 Select all the Favorites which should go into a particular folder (hold down Shift or Ctrl to select more than one at once). Click Move..., select the folder and click OK.

4 Click Close to finish organising your Favorites.

5 Your Favorites menu now has submenus. To access them, hold the mouse pointer over the folder's menu entry for a second or two. The submenu will appear, enabling you to select one of your Favorites.

Renaming and Deleting Favorites

You may also want to rename some of your Favorites, or delete the ones you're no longer interested in.

HANDY TIP

If you want your Favorites or folders to appear in a particular order, give them names beginning with 1, 2, 3 and so on.

1 To rename a Favorite, open the Organize Favorites dialogue box, select the Favorite and click Rename. Type in the new name and press Return.

2 To delete a Favorite, open the Organize Favorites dialogue box, select it and click Delete.

You can access the Favorites in a folder by double-clicking on it (use the Up One Level ⬆ button to return to the main listing). The same procedures can also be used to rename or delete folders. Deleting a folder also deletes its contents.

Finding Out the URLs of Your Favorites

The Organize Favorites dialogue box also enables you to check the URL of a Favorite.

HANDY TIP

You may find it easier to use the Windows file management utility, Explorer, to organise your Favorites. They are kept in a Favorites folder within your Windows folder, and you can move, copy or delete them just as you would any other file.

1 Open the Organize Favorites dialogue box and right-click on the Favorite. Select Properties from the pop-up menu.

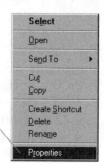

2 The Internet Shortcut section of the Properties box lists the URL.

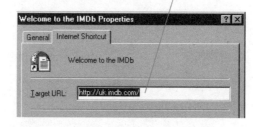

3 To copy it into a letter or report, select it and press Ctrl+C. Switch to your word processor and press Ctrl+V to paste it into the current document.

Internet Shortcuts

An Internet Shortcut is a Favorite which lives on your Desktop, rather than in the Favorites menu. Double-clicking on it connects you to the Internet, runs Internet Explorer and takes you to the specified page.

Internet Shortcuts are useful if there are a handful of sites which you visit regularly. For example, you might use a Shortcut to a news site, such as the PA News Centre (see page 69), to start Internet Explorer in the morning. Later in the day you might want to use a search engine or go straight to a sports or entertainment site.

I   To create an Internet Shortcut for the current page, select Create Shortcut from the File menu, or from the pop-up menu which appears when you right-click on the page.

File	
New Window	Ctrl+N
Open...	Ctrl+O
Save	Ctrl+S
Save As File...	
New Message...	
Send To	▶
Page Setup...	
Print...	Ctrl+P
Create Shortcut	
Properties	
Close	

2   A dialogue box appears; click OK to confirm the creation of the Shortcut.

3   The Shortcut is placed on your desktop. Double-click on it to start Internet Explorer and load the specified page (if Internet Explorer is already running, double-clicking on a Shortcut simply takes you to the page, just as selecting a Favorite would).

The PA NewsCentre

Customising the Links Bar

You can add five of your favourite pages to the Links bar, replacing the five default sites (generally five Microsoft sites, although your service provider or company may provide a customised version featuring other sites).

1 To add the current page to the Links bar, select Options... from the View menu.

2 Click on the Navigation tab.

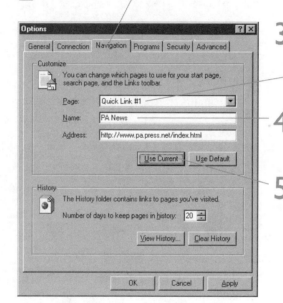

3 Select one of the Links from the drop-down list.

4 Give your Link a (short) name.

5 Click Use Current to copy the page's URL into the Address box.

HANDY TIP

If you know the URLs of your five sites, you can simply type them in. It isn't quite as easy as clicking the Use Current button, but it does enable you to customise the Links bar without connecting to the Internet.

6 Click OK to finish, then browse to the next of your five sites and repeat the process.

7 A single click on one of the five buttons takes you directly to that site.

The Start Page

The Start Page is the page Internet Explorer looks for each time you run it; it's also the page you are taken to when you click the Home button or select Start Page from the Go menu.

The default Start Page is usually the Internet Explorer Start Page on Microsoft's Web site, although you may be taken to one of your service provider's pages instead. You don't have to stick with the default settings, though – you can change the Start Page to any page you visit often or find useful, such as a news site or a Web directory.

Remember that the Start Page isn't just the place where you begin each session; it's also a page you can get back to easily. A page you visit often may be a more practical choice than the site you go to first (remember, you can use a Shortcut to override the Start Page and send Internet Explorer to some other site – see page 49).

HANDY TIP

If you know the URL, you can just type it into the Address box.

1 To make the current page your Start Page, select Options… from the View menu and click on the Navigation tab.

2 Check that Page: is set to Start Page and click Use Current.

3 Click OK.

The Search Page

Clicking Search, or selecting Search the Web from the Go menu, takes you to the Search Page.

You can also search Yahoo! (see page 66) **by typing two or more words, separated by spaces, into the Address bar and pressing Return. Internet Explorer realises your words aren't a URL, so it initiates a search.**

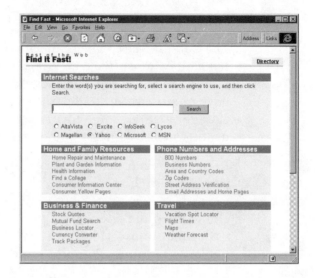

A search engine enables you to search or 'query' a vast database containing information about millions of Web pages. These databases are updated automatically as new pages are added to the Web.

The default Search Page usually enables you to try a selection of the most popular search engines. Type the word or words you're looking for into the box, choose a search engine and then click the Search button to see a list of 'hits' – pages which include your word(s). You can then follow the links to check out the most promising sites.

This page makes it easy to compare the various engines and decide which one works best for you. However, you'll get better results by searching from the home site of your favourite engine (see page 67 for some addresses), because then you can read the instructions and take advantage of any special features.

Like the Start Page, the Search Page can be customised, so once you've decided which engine you like best, you can configure Internet Explorer to go straight to it.

Follow the instructions on the previous page, selecting Search Page from the Page: drop-down list before you click Use Current.

Searching Tips

Searching the Internet can be frustrating at first, but with a little practice it's possible to locate information quickly and efficiently.

1 Decide whether you're searching or browsing. If you're looking for general information about a broad topic, such as 'ice skating', use a hierarchical directory, such as Yahoo!, to find sites which concentrate on that subject. If you're looking for a specific person or event, use a search engine.

HANDY TIP

Don't be surprised if a search engine finds a few pages which can't be reached. The Internet is very volatile and pages come and go daily.

2 Read the instructions. The popular search engines all have slightly different options, and what works with one won't necessarily work with another. Once you've found an engine you like, stick with it – the others may find a slightly different selection of sites, but you won't miss much.

3 Think words, not concepts. Most search engines simply find documents containing the words you specify, so don't try to describe the concept – you'll get better results by thinking of terms which are likely to appear in the text.

4 Refine your search with phrases and extra terms. Most engines allow you to specify that two or more words should appear together, or that the documents must contain some words and not others. Searching for 'John' and 'Smith' finds around 400,000 sites; searching for the phrase 'John Smith' brings it down to 7,000; and searching for 'John Smith' plus 'Labour' gives you 150 hits, the majority of which deal with the late politician.

5 Use alternatives. Try 'movie' as well as 'film', and don't forget that 'football' is 'soccer' to many people.

The History Folder

If there's any chance you might want to return to a page, it's a good idea to make a Favorite or Shortcut for it, because deleting the ones you don't use is much easier than retracing your steps. However, all isn't lost if you haven't – you can use the History folder to return to any page you've visited in the last couple of weeks.

1. Select Open History Folder from the Go menu to see where you've been.

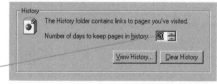

2. Sort the list by Title, Internet Address or the date it was Last Visited by clicking on the grey buttons across the top of the window. Click again to reverse the sort order.

HANDY TIP

Web authors don't always give their pages meaningful titles, so it can be hard to find the one you want. Sorting the entries by date makes things easier.

3. When you've found the page you want to return to, double-click on its title.

You can specify how long information should remain in the History folder. Don't get carried away, though – the more you have in there, the harder it is to find the page you want.

HANDY TIP

The Options dialogue box also enables you to empty the History folder and start again – just click the Clear History button.

1. Select Options… from the View menu and click on the Navigation tab.

2. Use the up and down arrows to adjust the number of days the information remains in the History Folder.

3. Click OK.

CHAPTER FIVE

Downloading Files

Pages, images, sounds and videos are easy to work with because they can all be loaded directly into Internet Explorer. This chapter explains how to deal with files which Internet Explorer can't display, such as program files, archives and unusual data files.

Covers

Understanding File Extensions

HANDY TIP

UNIX and Apple Macintosh files can have longer file extensions, such as gtar and html. The html files won't give you any trouble, but it's best to avoid anything else with a long extension.

File extensions are three-letter 'tags' which appear at the end of most file names, enabling you to work out what kind of file you're dealing with. Windows doesn't always display them, but you'll find it much easier to work with the Internet if you turn them on and learn to recognise the most common ones.

To display file extensions, run the file management utility Explorer and select Options... from the View menu. Make sure the Hide MS-DOS file extensions... box is unchecked.

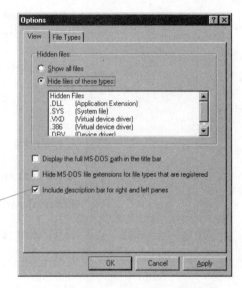

The file extensions you're most likely to encounter on the Internet are:

HANDY TIP

Plain text (.txt) files are down-loaded into the main window. They don't contain any formatting information, so they always look pretty drab.

Extension	Type of File	See Page
txt	Plain text document	–
rtf	Formatted text document	110
doc	Text or MS Word document	110
htm, html	Web page	–
pdf	Adobe Acrobat document	61
exe	Program or self-extracting archive	57
zip	Archive	60
gz, Z, tar, gtar	UNIX archives (avoid)	–
hqx, sit, sea	Apple Macintosh archives (avoid)	–
avi, qt, mov, mpg	Video clip	39
gif, jpg	Image	34
wav, au, snd, aif	Sound sample	39
ra, ram	RealAudio sound	41

Downloading Program Files

There's lots of software available on the Internet, including public domain and shareware programs, demo versions of commercial software and add-ons for many programs. Internet Explorer enables you to download and run these files in a single operation, but you'll almost always want to save them on to your hard disk instead. You can then experiment with your new software once you've disconnected from the Internet.

HANDY TIP

The files shown here can be downloaded from Microsoft's Web site – see page 64.

1   To download a program (.exe) file, click on the appropriate link.

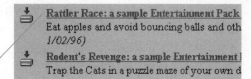

2   Internet Explorer begins to download the file.

BEWARE

There's always a chance that a downloaded program might contain a virus. See page 116 for details.

3   After a few seconds it asks whether you want to open (run) the file or save it on to your hard disk. Choose Save it to disk, then click OK.

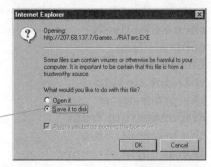

4   The standard Save As dialogue box appears. Select a folder and click Save.

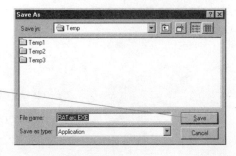

...contd

5 The file is then downloaded on to your hard disk – this often takes several minutes. You can continue browsing while it downloads, or switch to another application and carry on working.

6 The file ends up in the folder you specified. Once you've logged off, you can locate and run it.

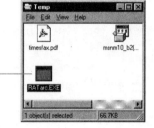

Opening Files

If you're upgrading Internet Explorer, or downloading an extra component which you want to use immediately, you can open the file instead of saving it on to your hard disk.

1 Click on the link as before, but select Open it rather than Save it to disk when you reach step 3.

2 When the download is complete, you receive a second security warning. If the program has been digitally signed (see opposite), you are shown its certificate. If it hasn't, you're warned that it is of unknown origin. Either way, click Yes to continue or No to abort.

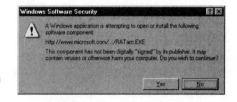

3 If you choose Yes, the file is opened (run) and the upgrade or component is installed.

HANDY TIP

You can upgrade Internet Explorer, or install add-ons such as ActiveX controls (see Chapter Nine), without closing the program or disconnecting from the Internet. This seems quite strange the first time you try it, but it works very well.

58   **Internet Explorer in easy steps**

Authenticode

Authenticode technology enables developers to add a 'digital signature' to their software. These signatures are the on-line equivalent of the holograms attached to Microsoft's software boxes – they demonstrate that the application is genuine.

The signature takes the form of a certificate which verifies the identity of the publisher of the program. The presence of a certificate also proves that the program hasn't been tampered with, so you can install it with confidence.

If you select Open it rather than Save it to disk when you download a program file, you will be shown its certificate once it has downloaded. If it's unsigned, you'll get a warning message instead – see the previous page.

If you've saved a file to disk, you have to open it from within Internet Explorer to see its certificate.

see the previous page.

HANDY TIP

Running a program from within another program may seem a bit weird at first, but that's exactly what you're doing when you use the 'regular' version of Explorer to open files.

1 Select Open from the File menu and click the Browse button.

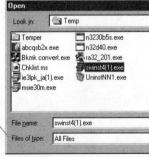

2 Make sure Files of type: is set to All Files, then locate the file. Click Open and OK.

3 When you're asked what you'd like to do, select Open it rather than Save it to disk. You'll see its certificate or be warned that it doesn't have one.

Compressed Files

Web page authors often use compression programs to 'archive' the program files linked to their pages. There are two reasons for this:

- Most programs consist of several files – there may be a setup utility and help files as well as one or more .exe files. Creating an archive keeps them all together.

- The resulting archive is often substantially smaller than the original group of files, so it downloads more quickly.

You'll also come across self-extracting archives – these have an .exe extension and unzip themselves when you run them.

The most popular compression program on the PC, PKZIP, produces archives with a .zip extension. Follow the instructions on pages 57–8 to save them on to your hard disk.

Once you have downloaded a .zip file, you'll need to decompress or 'unzip' it. There are numerous shareware unzippers, but PKZIP for Windows is the best choice for beginners. You can get a copy from PKWARE's Web site at: http://www.pkware.com/

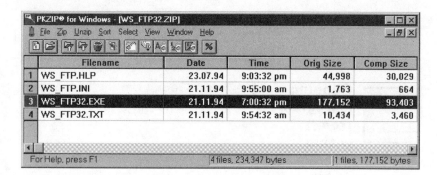

Unusual Data Files

HANDY TIP

PDF stands for Portable Document Format. Like Web pages, PDF files can contain text, illustrations and hypertext links, but the formatting and layout can be more complex. You view them using Acrobat Reader, which is available from Adobe's Web site – see page 83.

You'll come across some data files which a default installation of Internet Explorer can't display, such as Adobe Acrobat (.pdf) files.

1 As always, you start the download by clicking on a link.

2 If you have an application which can display the file, Internet Explorer asks whether you want to Open it or Save it to disk.

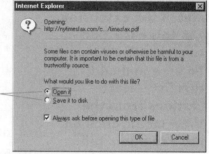

3 If you select Open, the file is automatically transferred to an appropriate application – in this case Acrobat Reader.

HANDY TIP

TimesFax is a mini-edition of *The New York Times* **in PDF format** – see page 70 for details.

4 You can then read or print the file (if it's a lengthy document, you'll probably want to log off temporarily). Once you've finished, close Acrobat Reader and switch back to Internet Explorer.

...contd

 HANDY TIP

When you try to download an unusual file, Internet Explorer uses the File Types list to match the extension – in this case .pdf – to an application. To view and edit this list, select Options from the View menu, click on the Programs tab and then click the File Types button.

5 If it can't find a suitable application, Internet Explorer gives you an 'unknown type' message. If you select Open it..., you'll be asked which

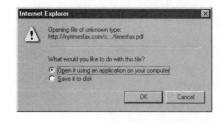

program it should use. Chances are, though, that you don't have anything which can load this type of file, so you should either save it (you'll then need to obtain an application which can display it) or cancel the transfer.

Most sites which use unusual file formats include a link to a site containing the software you require. If you download and install the software before you try to download the files, you shouldn't have any problems following steps 1 to 4.

Microsoft's ActiveX Document technology (see page 110) makes it possible for other software vendors to create add-on viewers for Internet Explorer, enabling you to display unusual data files in the main window. Adobe was developing an add-on version of Acrobat Reader at the time of writing, so by now you may be able to view PDF files without switching applications. It seems likely, however, that there'll always be some data files which can only be displayed using an external program.

CHAPTER SIX

Exploring the Web

The Internet has so much to offer that it's hard to know where to start. The best way to learn about the Web is by exploring it, so here's a selection of useful, interesting and entertaining sites which provide a good introduction.

Covers

Microsoft

Microsoft
http://www.microsoft.com/

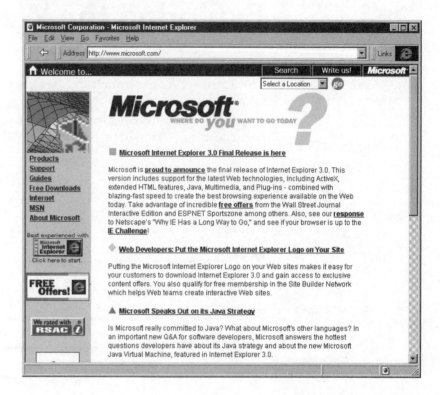

Microsoft's Web site is much like Microsoft itself – huge. There's lots of information about the company's products, including Windows, Office, the many multimedia CD-ROMs and, of course, Internet Explorer. You can also download demos and add-ons, or access the Knowledge Base for answers to technical questions and 'how-to' articles that help you get more from your software.

MSN

The Microsoft Network
http://www.msn.com/homemsn/

Also accessible from the Internet Explorer Start Page, the MSN site consists of hundreds of professionally presented information and entertainment pages. Sections include MSNBC, a customisable news service; Slate, an on-line magazine; and CarPoint, a car-lovers paradise. Music Central is a spin-off from the CD-ROM of the same name, as is the Cinemania section, and you'll also find pregnancy and childcare, kids and finance areas, plus a couple of interactive comedy/dramas. The pages take advantage of many of Internet Explorer's innovative new features, and it's all done with Microsoft's usual flair.

Directories

Yahoo!
http://www.yahoo.com/

Most of the sites featured in this chapter are large, well-established and unlikely to move or vanish. If you do find that one of the addresses is no longer valid, you may still be able to find the site using a directory or search engine.

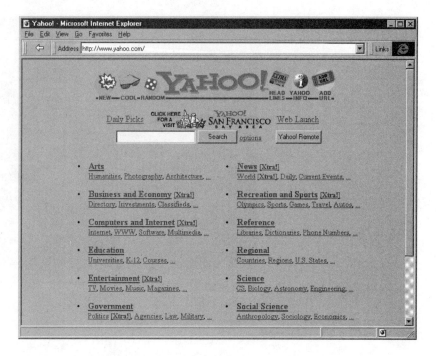

Yahoo! is a hierarchical directory of Web pages and (some) other Internet resources. Each of the 14 categories is progressively subdivided into more tightly defined subcategories, enabling you to work your way down to a list of Web sites which concentrate on your area of interest. It's extensively cross-referenced and very easy to use.

You could also try:

YELL, a UK Web directory brought to you by Yellow Pages. It's nowhere near as comprehensive as Yahoo!, but it's handy if you're looking for UK sites. Find it at:
http://www.yell.co.uk/

Search Engines

Alta Vista
http://www.altavista.digital.com/

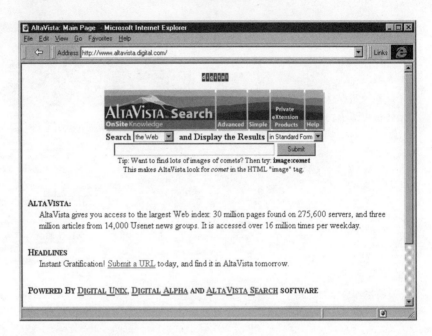

HANDY TIP **If you're new to the Web, or exploring a broad subject area, use one of the directories; if you want to find a specific piece of information quickly, use a search engine.**

Alta Vista enables you to search for Web sites and Usenet newsgroups containing a particular word or phrase. It takes some practice to get the best out of it – it's easy to make your search too broad, producing thousands of hits – but it does enable you to find information very quickly.

You could also try:
Lycos, which provides a very similar service, although it doesn't cover newsgroups. Lycos also offers a Yahoo!-style hierarchical directory, a2z. Find it at:
http://www.lycos.com/

Best and Worst

Point
http://www.pointcom.com/gifs/home/

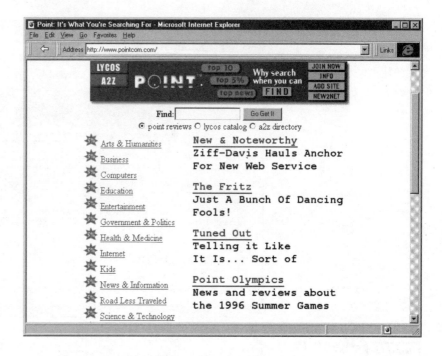

There are many amusing, unusual and downright odd sites on the Web. These services will help you track them down.

A sister site to Lycos (see page 67), Point reviews and rates the top five per cent of Web sites. Its listings are a good place to start if you find the all-embracingness of Yahoo! (see page 66) daunting.

You could also try:

Cool Site of the Day, for a daily pointer to a site worth your attention, at:
`http://cool.infi.net/`

Useless World Wide Web Pages, for an overview of all things pointless, at:
`http://www.chaco.com/useless/`

News

PA NewsCentre
http://www.pa.press.net/

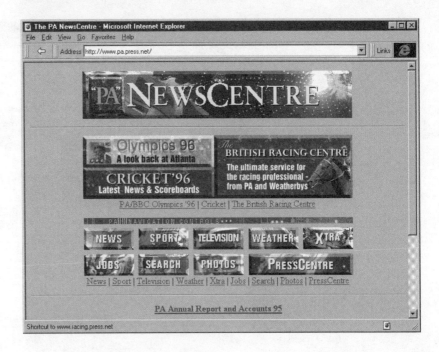

HANDY TIP

Many large sites require you to register before you can access any of the information - see page 97.

The PA NewsCentre site draws on the information gathered by the Press Association's news agencies. You get news headlines on the hour, a roundup of the day's papers, sports news, television and radio schedules and weather forecasts. There's generally more breadth than depth, but it's good for an up-to-the-minute overview.

You could also try:

The Electronic Telegraph, which provides everything you'd expect from a 'proper' paper, including cartoons and a crossword. You can also search the archives, which go back to November 1994. Find it at:
`http://www.telegraph.co.uk/`

The Times is also on-line, complete with classified ads, crosswords and news updates throughout the day. Find it at:
`http://www.the-times.co.uk/`

CNN Interactive
http://www.cnn.com/

One of the great things about the Internet is the tremendous choice of viewpoints. Rather than sticking to British news sites, for example, why not pop over to the States for an American perspective on US and world news? CNN's site provides a wide range of clearly presented, cross-referenced stories, plus a searchable archive.

You could also try:

USA Today, the on-line version of the USA's biggest-selling general interest paper. Find it at:
`http://www.usatoday.com/`

TimesFax, an eight-page mini-edition of the *New York Times,* distributed as an Adobe PDF file (see page 61). Browse through it on your screen or print it out to read in comfort. Find it at:
`http://nytimesfax.com/`

Points of View

PoliticsNow
http://www.politicsnow.com/

PoliticsNow reports on and analyses the American political situation. It aims to provide a balanced view of the issues and enables voters to pose questions and register their opinions. UK readers can follow the links to other on-line resources for more information about the American political system. Sadly, there isn't – as yet – a UK equivalent.

You could also try:

The Conservative Party, at:
`http://www.conservative-party.org.uk/`

The Labour Party, at:
`http://www.poptel.org.uk/labour-party/`

The Liberal Democrats, at:
`http://www.libdems.org.uk/`

HotWired
http://www.hotwired.com/

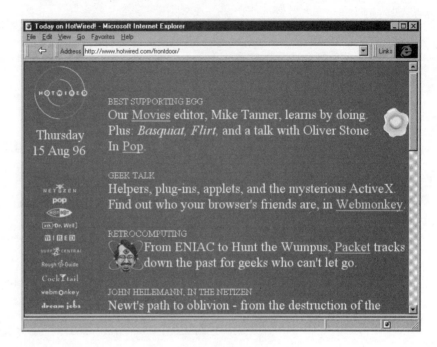

 On-line magazines are often referred to as 'e-zines'. Some e-zines have paper equivalents, but many exist only on the Web.

The US version of *Wired* magazine reflects and shapes Internet culture; HotWired is its on-line offshoot. It covers politics, popular culture, technology and the Internet, and takes itself very seriously. HotWired can be somewhat impenetrable, but it's tremendously authoritative.

You could also try:
For a UK perspective on the Internet, try the on-line versions of *.net* and *Internet*. Find them, respectively, at:
`http://www.futurenet.co.uk/netmag/net.html`
`http://www.emap.com/internet/`

Women's Wire
http://www.women.com/

Women's Wire is an intelligent e-zine aimed primarily at career women. Sections include news, entertainment, careers, style and health & fitness, and you can e-mail questions to the site's panel of experts. The presentation is very professional and it's a good read.

You could also try:

A Man's Life, a men's magazine which provides "complete instructions for health and wealth". It's less career-oriented than Women's Wire and covers everything from women and clothes to money and sport. Find it at:
`http://www.manslife.com/`

Entertainment

The Internet Movie Database
http://uk.imdb.com/

The Internet Movie Database contains pretty much everything you're likely to want to know about over 70,000 movies. As well as providing cast lists, synopses and reviews, it has links to everything from official studio sites to fan pages for directors and actors.

You could also try:

Most studios and distributors have extensive sites. Try:

MCA/Universal Pictures, at: http://www.mca.com/
MGM/UA, at: http://www.mgmua.com/motionpictures/
Miramax, at: http://www.miramax.com/
Paramount, at: http://www.paramount.com/
Walt Disney, at: http://www.disney.com/

YELL (see page 66) has a film-finding service with programme details for 450 UK cinemas.

The BBC
http://www.bbcnc.org.uk/

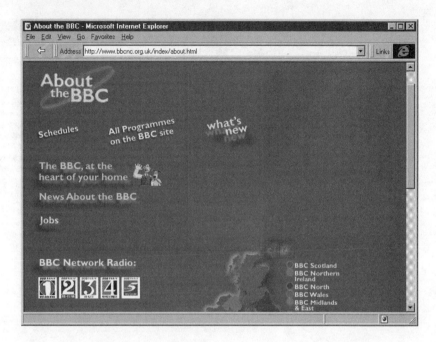

Aunty Beeb's site has back-up material for a selection of television and radio programmes, including *Blue Peter, Watch Out, Woman's Hour* and *The Net*. You can also find out what's on the box – or the air – this week.

You could also try:

Channel 4, for listings and links to programme-related sites. Find it at:
`http://www.channel4.com/`

Sky Internet, an extensive Web site with schedules, news, sport and programme-related material. Find it at:
`http://www.sky.co.uk/`

Many popular programmes have their own Web sites. Use Yahoo! or YELL (see page 66) to find your favourites.

Grooves
http://pathfinder.com/grooves/

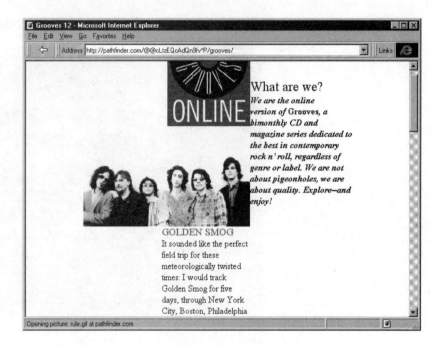

It's hard to find a music site with something for everyone, but Grooves comes pretty close. It concentrates on contemporary rock and combines well-written commentary with sound samples and attractive graphics.

You could also try:

Virgin Radio, complete with RealAudio broadcasts, at:
`http://www.virginradio.co.uk/`

Jazz Online, an interactive publication specialising in jazz, blues, new age and world music. Find it at:
`http://www.jazzonln.com/`

Classic CD, for extracts from the magazine of the same name, a beginner's guide to classical music and a list of music-related Web sites. Find it at:
`http://www.futurenet.co.uk/music/`
`classiccd.html`

Sport

Soccernet
http://www.soccernet.com/

Soccernet provides news, results, league tables, match reports, gossip and lots of football trivia. It concentrates on the Premier League and has extensive information pages for the top 16 teams, but gives results for all the English and Scottish divisions.

You could also try:

CricInfo, the self-styled "home of cricket on the Internet". Based, surprisingly, in the United States, it covers all international, first-class and one-day domestic cricket worldwide and provides news, scorecards, match reports, statistics, player profiles and other cricket-related information. Find it at:
http://www.cricket.org/

National Basketball Association
http://www.nba.com/

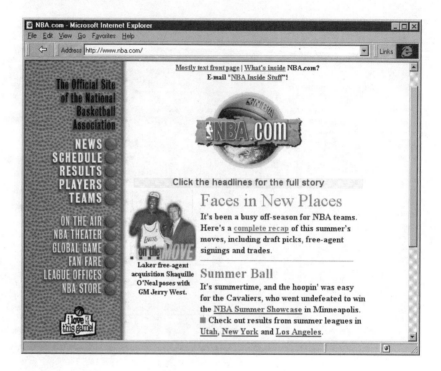

Having access to the Internet makes it easy to follow sports which don't get a lot of coverage in the UK. The NBA site features sound samples, video clips and interviews as well as news, previews, results and profiles, and while it isn't quite as good as being there, it's a truly excellent site.

You could also try:

Fastball, for Major League baseball, at:
`http://www.fastball.com/`

Skating the Infobahn, for links to in-line skating sites, at:
`http://www.skatecity.com/Index/`

t@p Extreme Sports, for climbing, mountain biking, skating, skiing and snowboarding:
`http://taponline.com/tap/sports/extreme/`

Home and Hearth

Electronic Gourmet Guide
http://www.2way.com/food/egg/

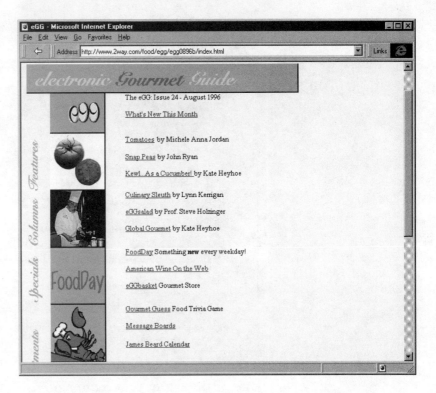

eGG is a well-established culinary e-zine featuring articles, columns, recipes, tips and food trivia. It's American, so you may need to 'translate' some of the ingredients, but the leisurely writing style makes it an enjoyable read.

You could also try:

The Rec.Food.Recipes Archive, which contains hundreds of recipes from the newsgroup of the same name. Find it at: http://www.cs.cmu.edu/~mjw/recipes/

The Virtual Garden
http://pathfinder.com/vg/

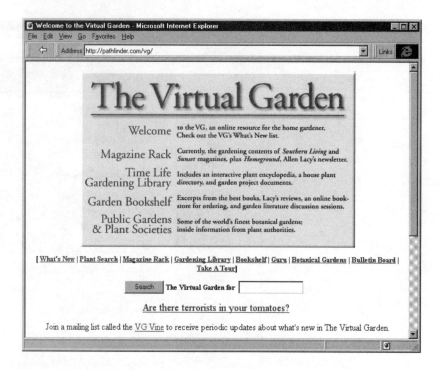

One of the many subsections of Time Warner's Pathfinder site, The Virtual Garden features extracts from various magazines, book reviews and information from the New York Botanical Garden and the American Orchid Society. Its best feature, though, is the gardening library, which comprises a searchable database of plants, a house plant database and a collection of project sheets.

Museums

Natural History Museum
http://www.nhm.ac.uk/

As well as providing information about opening times and current exhibitions, The Natural History Museum's site enables you to go behind the scenes and find out about some of the museum's on-going research projects. The interactive science casebooks are particularly impressive and should appeal to most children.

You could also try:
The Science Museum, at:
http://www.nmsi.ac.uk/

Portico, the British Library's on-line information service, at:
http://portico.bl.uk/

Science

Planet Science
http://www.newscientist.com/ps/

Planet Science is an offshoot of *New Scientist* magazine. You don't need to be a boffin to enjoy it, because it's written in layman's language and has plenty of material on the science of everyday life – including the answers to vexing questions like how long to leave a fizzy drink after you've shaken the can. You'll also find news, features, reviews and comment from the magazine.

You could also try:

The NASA Home Page, gateway to a vast collection of information about space and space exploration. Highlights include the latest images from the Hubble telescope, day-by-day coverage of shuttle missions and a huge, searchable archive of space pictures. Find it at:
http://www.nasa.gov/

Computing

Adobe
http://www.adobe.com/

Graphics specialist Adobe has a colourful site which provides information about its products, and hints and tips for getting the most out of them. You can also find out more about PDF files – see page 61 – and download a copy of Acrobat Reader, Adobe's PDF viewer.

You could also try:

Macromedia, for information about the company's range of multimedia products, and for a copy of its must-have ActiveX control, Shockwave – see page 107. Find it at: `http://www.macromedia.com/`

Progressive Networks, for more information about RealAudio – see page 41. Find it at: `http://www.realaudio.com/`

Many other software companies have Web sites. Use Yahoo! or a search engine (see pages 66–7) to track them down.

Hewlett Packard
http://www.hp.com/

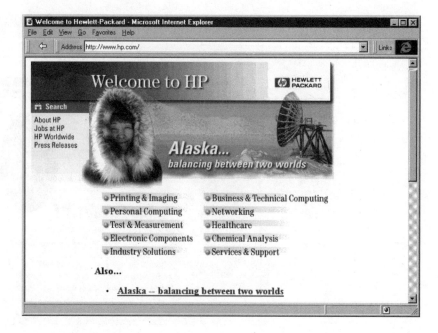

Hewlett Packard's site provides lots of information about the company's products, plus some interesting features. You can also download the latest software and drivers.

You could also try:

Most hardware companies have an on-line presence. For information about PC processors, try the Intel site at:
`http://www.intel.com/`

Gateway 2000, the computer manufacturer obsessed with black-and-white cows, has a fun site at:
`http://www.gw2k.com/`

You'll find lots of modem-related information at the home sites of the two best-known manufacturers:
Hayes, at: `http://www.hayes.com/`
US Robotics, at: `http://www.usr.com/`

Computer Manuals Online Bookstore
http://www.compman.co.uk/

With over 5,000 books, CD-ROMs and videos in its catalogue, Computer Manuals is one of Europe's largest mail order retailers of computer books. Once you've found a suitable title, you can order it on-line or by telephone.

You could also try:

Most publishers of computer magazines have Web sites, featuring excerpts and extra (generally Internet-related) material. Three of the biggest are:

Emap, at: `http://www.emap.co.uk/`
Future Publishing, at: `http://www.futurenet.co.uk/`
Ziff Davis, at: `http://www.zdnet.com/`

Use YELL (see page 66) to track down other publishers and individual magazines.

Service Providers

Direct Connection
http://www.dircon.co.uk/

Finally, don't forget to check out your service provider's Web site, which may provide technical support as well as details of its services. For example, my service provider, Direct Connection, maintains lists of Internet resources and useful starting points. You can also access the personal home pages of many of its members.

You could also try:

Check the information you were sent when you opened your account for the address of your service provider's site. Alternatively, inetuk maintains a list of providers in the UK and Ireland, with links to their Web sites. Find it at:
`http://www.limitless.co.uk/inetuk/`
`providers.html`

CHAPTER SEVEN

Intermediate Browsing

By now you know more than enough to make use of the Web, and you've probably spent some time exploring it. This chapter covers additional features which help you find what you're looking for, view foreign-language Web pages, learn something about the pages you've been looking at and browse more efficiently.

Covers

Finding Text

The Find command enables you to check whether a page contains a given word or phrase. It's useful when a search engine has taken you to a long page – rather than scrolling through it, you can jump straight to the relevant section.

1 To search for a word or phrase, select Find... from the Edit menu or press Ctrl+F.

3 Internet Explorer finds and highlights the text.

Entering part of a word can be more successful than entering the whole thing. For example, 'animat' finds 'animated' and 'animation'.

2 Enter a word or phrase in the Find dialogue box and click the Find Next button.

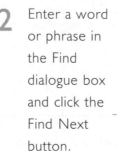

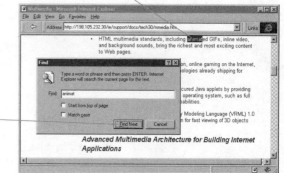

Advanced Multimedia Architecture for Building Internet Applications

You can move text from Internet Explorer to your word processor using the Copy and Paste commands. This is handy if you want to quote from a Web page in an article or project. It's also an easy way to make notes.

1 Drag the mouse over the text you want to copy. Select Copy from the Edit menu or press Ctrl+C.

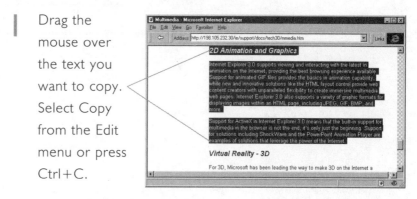

2 Switch to your word processor and select Paste from the Edit menu or press Ctrl+V.

Changing the Font Size

If you find the text on some Web pages difficult to read, you can easily make it larger.

1 To increase the size of the text, pull down the View menu and select Fonts, then select Large or Largest from the pop-up submenu.

HANDY TIP **You can also change the default fonts and the colour of the text – see page 112.**

2 Alternatively, click the Font button to cycle through the five available sizes.

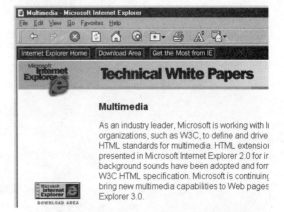

HANDY TIP **See page 94 to find out how to access the Technical White Paper shown in the screen grabs.**

3 If you're printing a Web page (see page 32), you might want to make the text smaller, so you can fit more on each page. Select a font size of Small or Smallest instead.

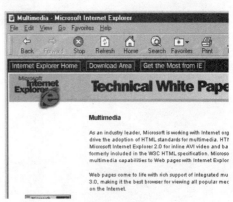

International

If you install the appropriate support pack, Internet Explorer can display pages written in Chinese, Japanese, Korean, Greek, Polish, Hungarian or any of the languages which use the Cyrillic alphabet.

1   To install foreign language support, connect to the Internet Explorer Home Page at:

    `http://www.microsoft.com/ie/`

2   Find your way to the download area, then download an International Support Pack from the additional features section. Once you've installed it, a 'globe and flags' icon is added to the right-hand end of the Status line.

3   Click on the icon and select the language you wish to use.

4   Log on to a site which uses that language – in this case, the home page of Microsoft Japan.

Viewing HTML Codes

Web pages are created using HyperText Mark-up Language, generally shortened to HTML. It's a two-step process: you write your text, then you insert HTML 'tags'. These tags tell Internet Explorer – or any other Web browser – how the text should be displayed, where to put the pictures and so on. Internet Explorer doesn't normally display these tags, but you can force it to do so if you're curious about HTML.

1 To see what the front page of the BBC's Web site (see page 75) 'really' looks like...

2 ...select Source from the View menu, or right-click on the page and select View Source from the pop-up menu. You can recognise the HTML tags because they are always surrounded by angled brackets < >.

HANDY TIP You can find out more about **HTML from Microsoft's Site Builder Workshop at:** http://www. microsoft.com/ workshop/.

```
bbcnc_org.htm - Notepad
File  Edit  Search  Help
<HTML>
<HEAD>
<TITLE>British Broadcasting Corporation</TITLE>
</HEAD>

<BODY BGCOLOR="#001042"  LINK="#214184" VLINK="#214184">

<CENTER><IMG SRC="/images/bbbc_1.gif" ALT="BBC" BORDER="0"></CENTER>
 <BR> <BR> <BR>
<CENTER>
<A HREF="index.html">
<IMG SRC="/images/anim3.gif" ALT="Animation" BORDER="1"></A></CENTER>
 <BR> <BR> <BR>
<CENTER>
<A HREF="/index/about.html"> <IMG SRC="/images/b_about.gif"  ALT="About the BBC" BORDER="0"></A>
                      
<A HREF="/index/progs.html"> <IMG SRC="/images/bprogs_1.gif" ALT="Programmes" BORDER="0"></A>
 </CENTER>

</BODY>
</HTML>
```

Reloading Pages

If a page hasn't downloaded properly, or a download has stalled, you can tell Internet Explorer to try again.

1   To reload the current page, click the Refresh button, select Refresh from the View menu or press F5.

HANDY TIP

If you think a download has stalled, check the modem icon ▭ **at the right-hand end of the Windows Taskbar. If the 'lights' stay red for more than 20-30 seconds, it's worth stopping the transfer and trying again.**

2   If Internet Explorer has connected to a site and then stalled halfway through the download, click the Stop button, select Stop from the View menu (or press Esc) to abort the transfer, then Refresh the page. This doesn't always work, but it's worth a try.

3   You'll also need to Refresh the current page if you've just turned on the images, sounds and videos (see page 43). You may sometimes have to do this after downloading an ActiveX control, too (see Chapter Nine).

4   Finally, you can use Refresh to make sure you're seeing the very latest version of a page. For example, pages showing sports results may be updated every few minutes, but the new data won't necessarily be sent to your computer, even though you're looking at the page. Sites which work this way generally instruct you to 'Reload often.'

New Windows

Internet Explorer allows you to have more than one main window open at once. For example, you might want to read an article in one window while you wait for an image-heavy page to download into another. Extra windows are also useful when you want to compare a saved page with an on-line one or keep a set of instructions in view.

I   To open a second window, select New Window from the File menu, or press Ctrl+N. The new window displays the current page.

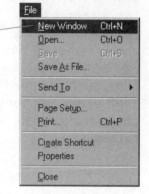

REMEMBER

The more you try to do at once, the slower everything gets, so avoid trying to download two or more image-heavy pages at once.

2   You now have two windows going at once. In this case the MSN Stock Market ticker is constantly scrolling across one while you read the latest MSNBC news in the other.

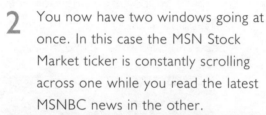

HANDY TIP

See pages 64-5 for details of Microsoft's many Web services.

3   Alternatively, you can send a linked page directly to a second window by right-clicking on the link and selecting Open in New Window.

Getting Help

HANDY TIP

Any file which is stored on your computer is said to be 'local'. Files stored elsewhere on the Internet are, from your point of view, 'remote'. You can access local files, such as saved Web pages, without connecting to the Internet.

Microsoft provides 'local' on-line help in the form of a standard Windows Help file. You'll also find a lot of useful information on its Web site, including beginner's guides, collections of frequently asked questions (FAQs), technical documents, and lots of hints and tips.

1   To access the local Help file, select Help Topics from the Help menu.

2   For more in-depth information, connect to the Internet and select Online Support from the Help menu. This option takes you to a page with links to a wide selection of useful resources.

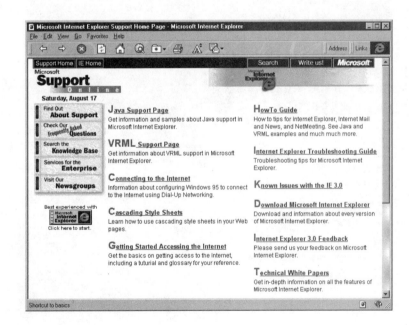

CHAPTER EIGHT

Interactive Web Pages

This chapter covers some of the ways that Web pages can be more than just a facsimile of a magazine or book page. Interactive elements, such as forms and animations, can make a page more useful, or just more fun to browse.

Covers

Forms

If you've explored some of the sites listed in Chapter Six, you've probably already encountered forms. They enable you to enter keywords into a search engine, fill out questionnaires and register for major sites.

Entering data into a form is just like using a dialogue box – you either fill in the blanks or select preset options using drop-down lists, radio buttons or check boxes. Once you have finished, you click a button to send the data back to the host computer. Generally you'll get a response, in the form of another Web page, in a few seconds.

For example, you can create a custom Start Page on MSN by filling in your details and specifying what you'd like to see when you log on.

HANDY TIP

Check boxes allow you to select several options at once, whereas radio buttons only allow you to select one. Radio buttons are used for mutually exclusive options, such as 'male' and 'female'.

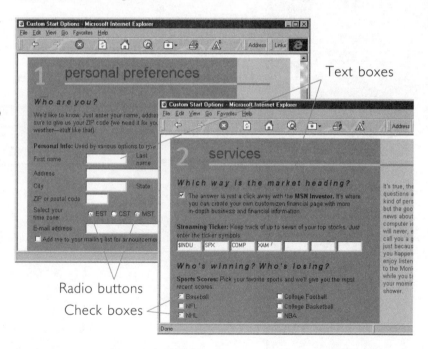

Text boxes

Radio buttons

Check boxes

Forms aren't always dry and serious; they are often used for interactive gadgets such as humorous questionnaires and automatic letter writers.

Site Registration

Many of the large commercial sites require you to register for access. This isn't as sinister as it sounds – usually the company concerned just wants to find out what kind of people use the site so it can sell advertising. While it's hard to get excited about the prospect of ads on Web pages, they do help fund services that you might otherwise have to pay for, such as the Electronic Telegraph (see page 69).

BEWARE

Don't ever use your log-on name and password, as supplied by your service provider, for site registration. Anyone who knows these details can use your Internet account, so keep them secret.

Registration involves filling in a form and selecting a user name and password. Unless you're feeling very paranoid, or planning to make credit card purchases over the Web, you can use the same user name and password for several sites. They really only serve to identify you, rather than to provide security. In many cases Internet Explorer can remember your details for you; on other sites you may be able to create a Favorite for the page after the registration page. You will occasionally need to enter the details yourself, though, so it's a good idea to write them down.

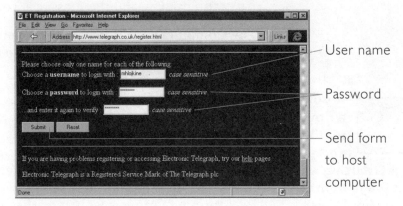

User name

Password

Send form
to host
computer

There are some sites which you can only get access to by paying a regular subscription, usually by credit card. Often you can find an equivalent site which doesn't charge for access, so don't be too quick to commit yourself. If you do decide to sign up for pay services, use a different password for each one, and keep those passwords secret.

Web Chat and Message Boards

Chat sites enable you to have a conversation – of sorts – with other Web users. It's more like passing notes in class than talking to someone face to face, though.

Chat pages have a form section at the top, where you enter your message, and a message area at the bottom, where the most recent messages are displayed. To join in, you simply type in a message and click the Send or Submit button. A few seconds later, your message is added to the bottom section, usually at the top of the list.

Some pages update automatically; others require you to click the Refresh button to see your contribution. More sophisticated sites use Java applets (see page 102) rather than forms, but the basic principles are the same.

With luck, someone responds to your message, you respond to theirs, someone else joins in... and you have a proper conversation. In practice, though, chat pages can be frustratingly slow and the messages correspondingly banal.

The Computers and Internet>Internet>World Wide Web> Communication section of Yahoo! (see page 66) has links to lots of chat pages.

 If you enjoy reading and contributing to message boards, you should also investigate Usenet newsgroups – see Chapter Thirteen.

Message boards, sometimes known as forums, are more like the letters page of a newspaper or magazine. Unlike chat sites, they aren't designed for real-time conversation – you just check back periodically to read any new messages, and perhaps add a response. They aren't quite as interactive as Web chat, but people sometimes get into long-running arguments, just as they do in letters pages.

News sites sometimes have message boards dedicated to current issues, and sports sites often provide a board where fans can discuss the performance of their teams.

Frames

Frames divide a Web page into several sections that can be scrolled or updated separately. It's a bit like having two or more separate pages squashed into the main window.

Clicking on a link can change the contents of the current frame, or one of the other frames, or take you to a completely separate Web page. Frames are often used for menus, mastheads and copyright notices.

For example, *People* magazine's Movie Reviews Database uses three frames. The top one has links to the site's interactive section and main page; the left-hand frame contains the index; and the reviews appear in the right-hand frame. Clicking on one of the letters at the top of the left-hand frame brings the appropriate section of the index into the bottom of that frame; clicking on a film name brings the review into the right-hand frame.

 You can find *People* magazine's Movie Review Database at: `http://pathfinder.com/people/movie_reviews/`

Most pages which use frames have grey dividing bars, but it's also possible for the author of the page to make the dividing bars invisible.

...contd

HANDY TIP

A page with frames can display material from more than one Web site. This enables Web authors to show you pages from other sites or take you on a guided tour.

Browsing a page with frames is similar to browsing a regular page, but there are a few things you should know.

1   Sometimes you can adjust the size of a frame by using the mouse to drag the dividing bar. If the mouse cursor changes into a double-headed arrow ↔ ↕ when you point at a bar, you can move it. If it doesn't, you're stuck with the frames as they are.

2   The Back command usually reverses the effect of your last action. Refresh returns all the frames to their original state (to Refresh an individual frame, right-click within it and select Refresh from the pop-up menu).

Saving and printing pages with frames is a bit tricky, because each frame is really a separate page.

3   To save the contents of a frame, click anywhere within it to select it, then select Save as File... from the File menu.

4   To print the contents of a frame, select it, then select Print... from the File menu or press Ctrl+P.

You can't tell which frame is selected by looking at the screen, so always click the one you want before you select Save or Print. If you want to preserve the appearance of the complete page, you can produce a screen grab like the one on the previous page:

5   Press Print Screen to copy the current screen image to the Windows Clipboard. Switch to a painting or image-editing program, such as Paint, and create a new document the same size as your screen display (probably 640x480 or 800x600 pixels). Select Paste from the Edit menu or press Ctrl+V to insert the image.

Client Pull and Server Push

Sometimes you'll download a Web page, only to have it suddenly disappear and be replaced with another one. You haven't done anything wrong; the first page has used 'client pull' to download the second one automatically.

Client pull is sometimes used to create welcome pages which stay on your screen for a few seconds, then give way to a menu page. It can also be used to redirect users when a site moves, to create automatic slideshows, or to update images or data at regular intervals.

You don't have to do anything to activate client pull – if a page includes a client-pull instruction, Internet Explorer will go looking for the next page, whether you want it to or not. It can be a bit disturbing the first time you come across it, but client pull is almost always either useful or entertaining. If you'd like to see it in action, use one of the search engines (see page 67) to look for pages containing 'client pull' or 'client-pull'.

Server push is the complement to client pull. In client pull the downloaded page requests or 'pulls' the new page; in server push the computer where the page is stored keeps sending or 'pushing' new files. Server push is usually used to update images, creating a 'flipbook animation' effect.

Internet Explorer 3.0 didn't support server push when it was released. This feature may be added at some point, but you won't be missing much if it isn't. Animated GIFs (see page 34) and Java applets (see overleaf) produce much smoother animations, so server push is almost certainly a dying technology.

Java Applets

Java is a programming language developed by Sun Microsystems. It enables Web authors to create small programs, or 'applets', which can be attached to Web pages. When you download the page, the applet is automatically downloaded and run.

Java is often used to add animated images to Web pages, and to create small games. You'll also come across some neat graphical effects, and it is sometimes used to create interfaces for Web chat (see page 98).

Unlike server-push animations, which arrive frame by frame, Java animations are downloaded completely before they are executed. Consequently they run smoothly, regardless of the speed of your connection, and can be a lot more sophisticated.

When you download a page with an attached applet, you'll see a blank rectangle, usually grey, in the area the applet uses. After a few seconds the rectangle is replaced by the animation or game (look out for 'Applet Loaded' and 'Applet Started' messages in the Status line). You don't have to start or stop the applet; you just watch or play, then move on to another page.

Java was designed with security in mind, but it's possible that a malicious programmer could use it to attack your machine. See page 116 to find out how to protect yourself.

You can tell Internet Explorer not to run Java applets. You might want to do this if you have a slow connection and it's taking a long time for them to download.

To turn off Java applets, select Options from the View menu and click on the Security tab. Uncheck the Enable Java programs box.

Active content

You can choose what type of software Web sites can download and run on your computer.

☑ Allow downloading of active content
☑ Enable ActiveX controls and plug-ins
☑ Run ActiveX scripts
☐ Enable Java programs   Safety Level...

CHAPTER NINE

ActiveX

ActiveX is a new software technology which enables Web
authors to create novel and innovative pages. This chapter
provides a bit of background and explains how to view
'activated' Web sites.

Covers

ActiveX Explained

ActiveX is an integration technology which enables software components to interact – or, in layman's language, a software 'glue' which can be used to stick bits of program together. Its three main applications are:

1   ActiveX Controls: If developers want to use special effects which Internet Explorer doesn't support, they can create add-on controls which increase its capabilities.

2   ActiveX Scripting: Developers can also use JavaScript or Visual Basic Script to create Web pages which respond to your actions. In this case the extra functionality is added to the page, rather than to your browser. ActiveX Scripting can also be used to integrate the behaviour of several ActiveX controls and/or Java applets (see page 102).

3   ActiveX Documents: If you have an appropriate application or viewer, you can view documents other than Web pages, such as Word files and Excel spreadsheets. The application's toolbar is added to Internet Explorer's main window, enabling you to edit the document.

ActiveX enables authors and programmers to create innovative Web sites with all the presentational flair and interactivity of multimedia CD-ROMs. They can also use it to customise a site to your individual preferences, or to develop powerful on-line applications, such as interactive catalogues and ticketing services.

ActiveX Controls

ActiveX controls are small pieces of software which add extra features to Internet Explorer, such as the ability to display scrolling messages. It's a bit like owning an electric drill: each time you encounter a new type of page (job), you simply download (buy) the necessary control (drill bit).

Each time you visit a Web page which uses ActiveX technology, Internet Explorer checks whether the required control has been installed on your system. If you don't have it, Internet Explorer installs it for you.

1 When you visit a page which requires an additional ActiveX control, you'll see an 'Installing components…' message in the Status line. The blue squares at the other end indicate the progress of the download.

You will get a second warning if the control uses data which may be unsafe.

2 If the control has been digitally signed (see page 59), you'll see its certificate; if it hasn't, you'll get a warning message. Click Yes to continue or No to abort the installation.

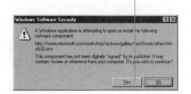

3 Once the control has been installed, you can view the active content of the page.

Examples of ActiveX Controls

The next three pages provide brief descriptions of a range of ActiveX controls. You'll find many of them in Microsoft's ActiveX Component Gallery, at:

`http://www.microsoft.com/activex/controls/`

Marquee (Microsoft)

The Marquee control scrolls text horizontally or vertically. It's often used to draw your attention to hot news stories.

Stock Ticker (Microsoft)

Tickers scroll real-time data, such as stock market figures or sports results, across a section of the page. They look like marquees, but the information is constantly being updated as the real-life situation changes.

Menu and Popup Menu (Microsoft)

These controls enable Web authors to attach menus to various items on a Web page, including buttons.

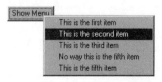

Chart (Microsoft)

This control enables Internet Explorer to draw charts. Downloading a few numbers is quicker than downloading an image of a chart, so it speeds things up considerably. It's also more flexible: if next week's numbers are different, Internet Explorer automatically draws an up-to-date chart.

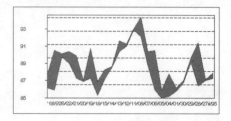

Shockwave (Macromedia)

The Shockwave control enables you to view multimedia presentations created with Director – an authoring package which is often used for multimedia CD-ROMs.

Shockwave presentations can include text, graphics, animation, digital video, sound and interactive elements. They can be very impressive – some of the most innovative material on the Web appears on 'shocked' sites.

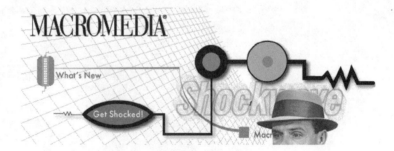

FutureSplash (Future Wave Software)

Animations created with FutureSplash – such as this typing seal – use a very compact file format, so they download quickly. Like Shockwave presentations, they can respond to the movement of the mouse pointer, as well as to any clicks you make.

Surround Video (Microsoft/Black Diamond)

The Surround Video control enables you to explore images created with a panoramic camera. They create the illusion that you're standing in the middle of the scene, spinning around in circles. You can stop at any point to admire the view, and in some cases you can also look up and down, or zoom in on part of the scene.

MSN's CarPoint section (see page 65) has Surround Videos of the interiors of several vehicles, including this Mercedes.

Earthtime (Starfish Software)

Earthtime shows you the local time in up to eight cities around the world, calculates time differences and shows you which parts of the globe are in darkness. It can even synchronise your computer's clock with one of the atomic clocks attached to the Internet.

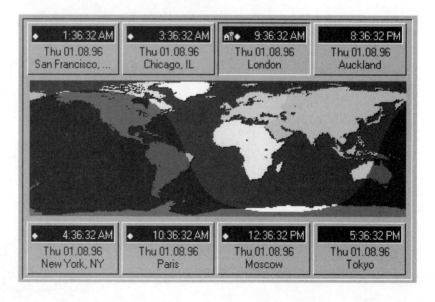

HANDY TIP

In the future, you'll be able to use ActiveX controls in other applications, too. You might add Surround Videos to your PowerPoint presentations, for example.

ActiveX Scripting

Scripts are mini programs which run within Internet Explorer's main window. They are used to create 'smart' Web pages which 'know' what to do when you click a button or enter some text. Common applications include games, simple utilities – such as loan calculators – and the checking of forms. They can also be used to place messages in the Status bar.

HANDY TIP

Internet Explorer supports both Visual Basic Script (VB Script) and JScript (Microsoft's implementation of JavaScript). The Visual Basic Script samples are at: `http://www.microsoft.com/vbscript/us/vbssamp/vbssamp.htm`

Scripts are embedded in the Web page, so you don't have to wait for them to download separately. They are also very responsive, because everything happens on your computer. If you're playing the hangman game from Microsoft's collection of sample scripts, for example, you can disconnect from the Internet as soon as you've downloaded the page, then play as many games as you want. The view keeps changing, but it's still the same page.

Developers can also use scripts to integrate Java applets and ActiveX controls.

```
vb script hangman
```

```
realm
you win!
```

		B	C				
G	H	I	J	K	F
	N	O	P	Q	
S	T	U	V	W	X
	Y	Z			
		Reset			

won: 1   lost: 0

ActiveX Documents

ActiveX Document technology enables you to view and edit documents other than Web pages, such as Word files and Excel spreadsheets. The application's menu and toolbars are added to the main window, giving you access to all its functions. It isn't quite the same as using the application on its own, though, because you can still use Internet Explorer's browsing functions (if you look closely at the screenshot, you'll see that the Button, Address and Links bars are still present).

 One of the good things about this technology is that any .doc or .rtf files you encounter are automatically opened in Word – within the main window. This means you can read these files without switching applications.

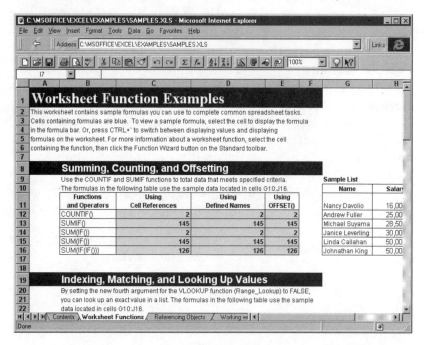

This only works with some programs, and the application must be installed on your computer. However, if you don't have the necessary software, you may be able to download a document viewer. Viewers for Word, Excel and PowerPoint are available from the Office Web site, at:
`http://www.microsoft.com/msoffice/`

ActiveX Document technology makes it possible to put existing files on to the Web without converting them into HTML. It could also be used to share documents across a company's internal network.

CHAPTER TEN

Personal Options

Fine-tuning the Options settings customises Internet Explorer to suit your way of working. This chapter covers most sections of the Options dialogue box and discusses the difficult question of Internet security.

Covers

General Options

The General Options section enables you to customise the presentation of Web pages.

1 Select Options from the View menu and click on the General tab.

REMEMBER

Changing the Colors and Links Options only affects pages where the author hasn't specified any colours.

2 See page 43.

3 Set colours for the text and the background of the main window.

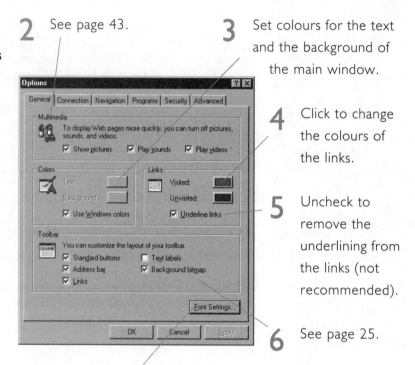

4 Click to change the colours of the links.

5 Uncheck to remove the underlining from the links (not recommended).

6 See page 25.

7 Change the default fonts. The proportional font is used for most Web page text, and can be anything you find easy to read. The fixed-width font is used for plain text documents, such as readme files, and sometimes for paragraphs pre-formatted by the author of a Web page. It's best to stick with Courier New – choosing another font may spoil the layout of some pages.

8 Click OK to confirm your choices, Cancel to abandon them or Apply to see how they will look.

Connection Options

The Connection Options control the way your computer accesses the Internet.

1 When this box is checked, Internet Explorer automatically brings up the Connect To dialogue box (see page 21) when you try to view something on the Internet.

2 If you have more than one account, use this drop-down list to specify which connection should be used. Click Properties to change your account details.

3 Tell Internet Explorer to drop the line if you don't seem to be doing anything.

4 Some service providers store all the pages users have requested recently on a proxy server, enabling you to access very popular pages more quickly. To make use of this service, check the Connect through… box, click the Settings button and enter the details supplied by your service provider. You may also need to use a proxy server if you are accessing the Web from a company network.

Programs Options

HANDY TIP

The Navigation section of the Options dialogue box is covered in Chapter Four, on pages 50-51.

The Programs Options are used to specify which of your other applications should be used for functions Internet Explorer can't handle.

1 Enter details of your e-mail and newsreading software – see Chapters Twelve and Thirteen.

2 Specify which programs should be used to view data files which Internet Explorer can't display – see pages 61-62.

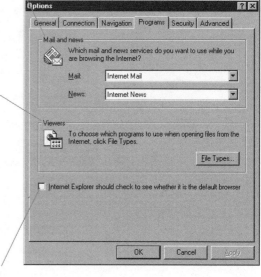

3 If you normally use another browser in preference to Internet Explorer, uncheck this box. Double-clicking on an Internet Shortcut will then start your alternative browser.

Internet Security

There are two aspects to Internet security: privacy, especially as regards credit card details, and protection of your machine, particularly from computer viruses.

Privacy

The Web hasn't been in use long enough for anyone to be sure how likely it is that your credit card details will fall into the wrong hands, but it's technically possible for Internet transmissions to be intercepted.

Consequently, companies which wish to sell products and services over the Internet often set up secure servers which use encrypted forms. If you're submitting an order to a secure site, you can be sure that your details are going to the right people, and will be protected from eavesdroppers along the way. The system isn't absolutely infallible, but it's probably more secure than ordering over the phone.

There are several ways to identify a secure site. The URL begins with https://, and a padlock icon 🔒 appears at the right-hand end of the Status bar. You can also view its security certificate.

In the future you will also need to be able to prove who you are, so that you can take advantage of on-line banking and other financial services. Digital IDs are the most likely solution: you'll be able to confirm your identity by transmitting a unique 'electronic signature'. Find out more from VeriSign at: `http://digitalid.verisign.com/`

1 To check the security status of a page, select Properties from the File menu. Click on the Security tab to see whether the site has a certificate.

2 You can also instruct Internet Explorer to warn you if you try to send data

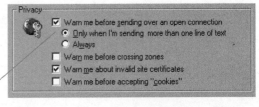

to an insecure site. Select Options from the View menu, click on the Advanced tab and check that the Warn me before sending... box is checked. Selecting Only when... rather than Always enables you to use search engines without getting a warning every time you submit a query.

Protection

You can only get a computer virus if you download and run an infected program. As well as checking all the software you download, you should be wary of programs attached to Web pages, such as Java applets and ActiveX controls. Other potential hazards include programs attached to e-mails, binary files posted to newsgroups (see Chapter Thirteen) and documents which may contain macros, such as Microsoft Word and Excel documents.

Software which is incomplete, badly written or simply incompatible with one of your applications can also interfere with the day-to-day operation of your system. The more you download, the more important it is to make backups.

It's a good idea to invest in some antivirus software – preferably the sort which examines everything which is saved on to your hard disk – and to have a regular schedule for backing up files which contain important information or would be difficult to replace. Download files from large, well-managed file archives (see Chapter Eleven) or directly from the company concerned, and be suspicious of anything sent to you by a stranger.

Internet Explorer also offers two levels of protection. Authenticode technology enables publishers to 'sign' their software, making it easier for you to decide whether an application or add-on is safe to install (see page 59). Alternatively, you can use the Security options to prevent Internet Explorer from running programs.

1   Select Options from the View menu, click on the Security tab and uncheck some or all of the Active content boxes.

2   Turn off animations, multimedia files and so on.

3   Turn off ActiveX controls.

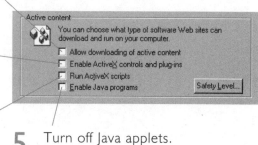

4   Disable any scripts which are downloaded.

5   Turn off Java applets.

Content Advisor

You can also use the Security Options to prevent your children from accessing 'adult' Web sites.

Ratings

At the time of writing, the vast majority of sites were unrated. Test your settings on a selection of 'undesirable' sites before you rely on them to protect your children from on-line violence or pornography.

Internet Explorer supports the Platform for Internet Content Selection (PICS) rating system. This means that Web authors can assess their sites according to criteria set by groups such as the Recreational Software Advisory Council (RSAC) and embed a rating in each page. Internet Explorer will then block access to pages with language, nudity, sex or violence ratings you consider unacceptable.

1. To turn on Ratings, select Options from the View menu. Click the Security tab, then click the Enable Ratings button.

2. Choose a supervisor password. You will need this password to change the Ratings settings.

Click on the General tab to access additional options. You can prevent users from viewing unrated sites or enable them to access restricted sites by entering the password.

3. Select a category and use the slider to select a rating. Repeat for the other three categories, then click OK.

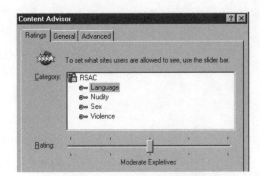

4. Users will not be able to access sites with unacceptably high ratings.

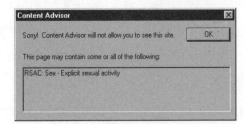

You can find out more about the ratings system from the RSAC Web site at:
`http://www.rsac.org/`

Advanced Options

HANDY TIP

To find out more about the options not covered in this chapter, click the question mark ❓ icon in the top right corner of the dialogue box, then click on the option you want more information about.

The most important section of the Advanced Options page is the one headed Temporary Internet files.

Pages, images and multimedia files which you have viewed are 'cached' – stored temporarily on your hard disk – so that Internet Explorer can load them quickly when you revisit a site. Once the cache is full, older items are thrown out as new ones are added.

1   To customise the operation of the disk cache, select Options from the View menu and click the Advanced tab.

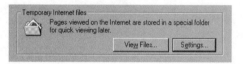

2   Click Settings.

3   Set Check for newer versions... to Every visit... if you want to be sure you're always seeing the most up-to-date version of each page. Selecting Every time... speeds things up without much loss of timeliness; Never gives the best performance, but some of what you see will be out of date.

4   Move the slider to the right if you have plenty of spare disk space, or to the left if you're running out of room.

5   To delete all the files in the cache, click Empty Folder. You might want to do this if you need extra disk space for another project.

CHAPTER ELEVEN

FTP and Gopher

As well as helping you access the Web, Internet Explorer enables you to make use of other Internet services, including FTP and gopher. This chapter explains how to download programs and documents from these sites.

Covers

FTP Explained

FTP stands for File Transfer Protocol, and it's a way of moving data from one computer to another. It isn't as popular as it used to be, mainly because the Web is more attractive and easier to use, but FTP sites are still used to store programs, documents and images. These sites are often referred to as 'archives', and you can think of them as the Internet equivalent of public libraries – except you don't have to return the files.

PD, Freeware and Shareware

Most of the software available from FTP sites is public domain, freeware or shareware. The first two can be used free of charge; the last is 'try before you buy' software. If you use a shareware program regularly, you have to pay a fee to the author. The fees are generally very reasonable and there is usually a reward for paying up or 'registering'. You might get a password which unlocks additional features, for example, or a printed manual. You'll find the details in the readme files associated with the program.

Basic Principles

Using an FTP site is much like locating a file on your hard drive – you simply work your way down through the folders (directories) until you find the file you're looking for. You can then download it to your computer. That's all there is to it, really – FTP doesn't have nearly as many bells and whistles as the Web.

Web pages occasionally link you directly to an FTP site, so it's handy to know how they work. If you want to spend a lot of time exploring FTP sites, you should get yourself a dedicated FTP program. Internet Explorer is okay for downloading a few files occasionally, but you can't upload files, and it isn't as flexible as a specialist FTP program.

Connecting to FTP Sites

Connecting to an FTP site is just like connecting to a Web page – you simply enter the address in the Address bar or Open dialogue box. The only difference is that FTP addresses begin with ftp:// rather than http://.

1 To connect to SunSITE at Imperial College (see page 123), select Open from the File menu, or press Ctrl+O, and type its address into the dialogue box.

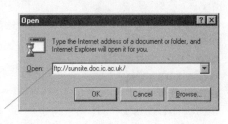

The welcome message often contains important information about the site. You should also look out for readme files – click on the file name to display the text in the main window. You can ignore any instructions about typing in commands, though – these are for people with specialist FTP applications.

2 A welcome message and a list of files and folders appear in the main window.

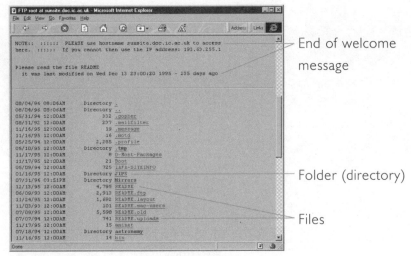

End of welcome message

Folder (directory)

Files

3 The files you can access will usually be a 'pub' folder – click on it to find out what it contains. Keep clicking on folders to move down the hierarchy. Use the Back button to work back up, or look for a Return… link at the top of the listing.

Downloading Files

The hardest part of using an FTP site is deciphering the file names. Look out for index files, which usually contain brief descriptions of all the files in a folder. Click on the file name to display the index in the main window.

Once you've found your way into the right folder and located an interesting file, it's very easy to download it to your computer.

1 To download a file, simply click on it with the mouse.

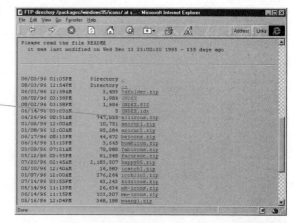

2 You receive the usual warning about viruses. Click Save it..., then click OK to bring up the standard Save As dialogue box.

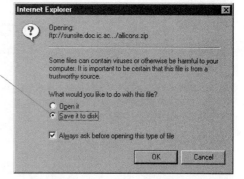

3 Select a folder and check the file name, then click Save. The file is downloaded on to your hard disk – this may take several minutes. Click the Cancel button if it's taking too long or you decide you don't want the file after all.

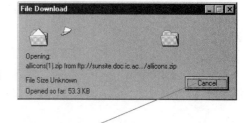

Useful FTP Sites

FTP addresses are usually written without the ftp://. If you see an address like: `ftp.funet.fi` **you may need to add the rest, giving:** `ftp://ftp.funet.fi/` **to enable Internet Explorer to find the site.**

SunSITE
ftp://sunsite.doc.ic.ac.uk/

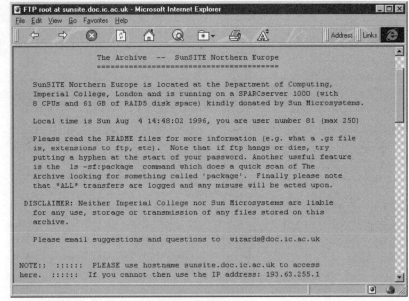

Many large FTP sites maintain up-to-date copies of sections of other sites. This is called 'mirroring', and it means you should be able to find most popular files on almost every large FTP site.

Based at Imperial College in London, SunSITE has space for over 60Gb of data. Unless you know exactly what you're looking for – and exactly where it is – it's best to start in the packages folder.

You could also try:

SUNET, a large user-friendly archive maintained by the Swedish University Network. Find it at: `ftp://ftp.sunet.se/`

Demon FTP, an archive maintained by the popular UK service provider. It isn't as vast as SunSITE, but you might find it easier to navigate. Start in the pub folder, then try ibmpc if you're looking for software. Find the site at: `ftp://ftp.demon.co.uk/`

Project Gutenberg
ftp://nptn.org/pub/e.texts/gutenberg/

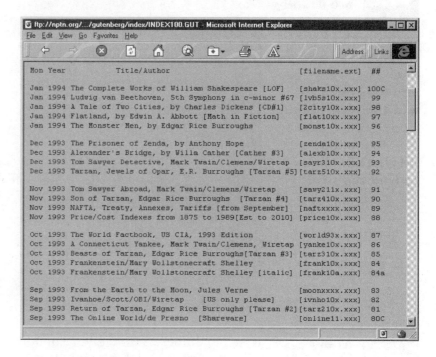

Project Gutenberg encourages people to create and distribute electronic versions of English-language texts. Most of the fiction dates back to last century, but you can also download electronic versions of reference works as diverse as The Complete Works of Shakespeare, The Bible, the first 100,000 prime numbers, Roget's Thesaurus, Abraham Lincoln's First Inaugural Address and The Communist Manifesto.

You could also try:

If you're looking for pictures, the Smithsonian's photograph collection covers art, science, technology, history and current events. It includes images from many of the museums on the Mall in Washington and can be found at:
`ftp://photo1.si.edu/`

Gopher Explained

Gopher sites look like FTP sites, but conceptually they have more in common with the Web, because they can give you access to files on several different computers. They use menus rather than folders and generally provide access to reports and documents rather than program files.

1 This is one of the University of Tasmania's gopher menus (see overleaf). Selecting the second item...

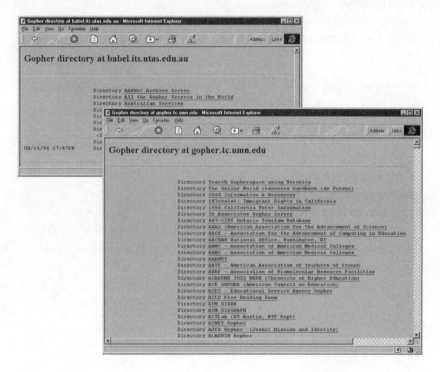

2 ...brings up this menu, which links you to many other gopher sites.

Unless you actively hunt them down – and it's hard to think of a good reason why you should – you won't come across many gopher sites. They've been pretty much superseded by the Web, which does the same job in a more user-friendly fashion.

Connecting to Gopher Sites

Like FTP addresses, gopher URLs are usually written without the gopher://. You may have to add this prefix before you type the address into the Open box.

Again, connecting to a gopher site is just like connecting to a Web page, except the address begins with gopher://.

1   To connect to the University of Tasmania's gopher site, select Open from the File menu, or press Ctrl+O,

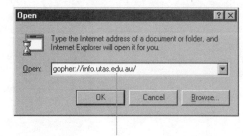

and type its address into the dialogue box.

You can create Favorites for FTP and gopher sites – simply select Add to Favorites... from the Favorites menu.

2   The site's main menu appears in Internet Explorer's main window. You can move to any sub-menu by clicking on it.

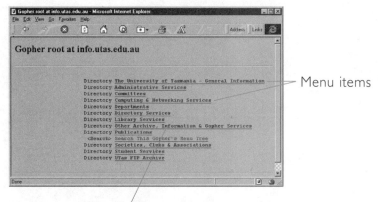

Menu items

3   Select the Other Archive... menu item to access the menus shown on the previous page.

CHAPTER TWELVE

Mail

Internet Mail enables you to send a message to anyone who is connected to the Internet.

Covers

E-mail Explained

E-mail is short for electronic mail, and it's the Internet equivalent of letters and faxes. It's better than either, though, not only because it's quick and cheap, but also because you can attach files to a mail message. This means you can send text documents, pictures, sound samples and program files as well as simple messages.

You can send mail to anyone on the Internet; you just need to know their address, which will look something like:

mhl@dircon.co.uk

The part before the @ is the recipient's user name.

The part after the @ is the address of the recipient's service provider.

When you send a mail message, it is delivered to the recipient's service provider very quickly – usually within a few minutes. It is then stored in the recipient's mail box until he or she next logs on and checks for new mail.

E-mail is very efficient if you're dealing with someone who checks their mail regularly, but not so good for getting messages to people who only log on once a week. It's also very handy for contacting people who are perpetually on the phone or out of the office, and it makes it easier to deal with people in different time zones – rather than calling at an awkward hour, you can have a message waiting for them when they arrive at work.

If you don't know someone's e-mail address, the easiest way to find it is by asking them. You can also try the on-line directories. The largest is Four11, at:
`http://www.four11.com/`

Installing Internet Mail and News

You can only use the Mail applet if your service provider supports SMTP/POP mail. If you're not sure about this, call up and ask. You'll also need to know the addresses of your provider's SMTP and POP3 servers and your user name and password (which may be different from the user name and password you use to log on).

Internet Explorer uses add-on applets for Mail and News. If they weren't supplied with your copy of Internet Explorer, you'll need to download them from Microsoft's Internet Explorer Web pages, at:
`http://www.microsoft.com/ie/`

1   Go to the Download area and look for an 'additional features' or 'extra components' link. Select Internet Mail and News from the list of add-ons and download the file.

2   Select Open it rather than Save it to disk (see page 58) to install the Internet Mail and News applets automatically.

3   You can run Internet Mail by selecting it from the Programs section of the Start menu, or from Internet Explorer. Select Read Mail from the Go menu, or click on the Mail button and select Read Mail (if this doesn't work, you need to make Internet Mail your default mail application – see page 132).

4   The first time you run Internet Mail, the Mail configuration Wizard appears and helps you enter your account details.

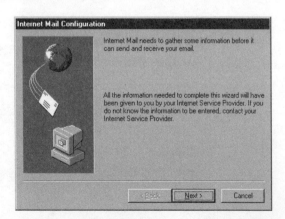

The Internet Mail Applet

Like Internet Explorer, Internet Mail has menu and tool bars across the top of the window, and a status bar at the bottom. However, the main window is normally divided into two 'panes', a message list pane and a preview pane.

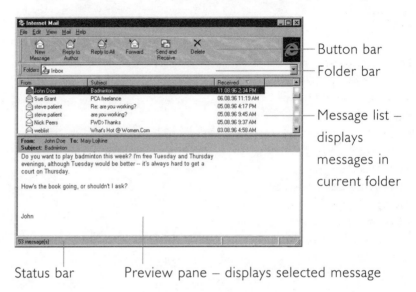

Button bar

Folder bar

Message list – displays messages in current folder

Status bar   Preview pane – displays selected message

The Button and Folder bars are collectively referred to as the Toolbar. The Folder bar enables you to select the Inbox, Outbox, Sent Items or Deleted Items folder, or any personal folders you have created – see page 136.

1   You can rearrange the Button and Folder bars by dragging their 'handles' – see page 25 – or use the View menu to turn off the Tool and/or Status bar.

2   You can also turn off the Preview pane, or swap the horizontal dividing bar for a vertical one.

Sending Mail

You have to be connected to the Internet to send a message, but you don't have to be on-line while you compose it. If you're concerned about your phone bill, log on, collect all your mail (see page 134) and log off. You can then read and reply to the messages at your leisure. Once you've done this – and composed any new messages – log on again and dispatch all your messages at once.

(see page 134)

You can send mail to yourself – just enter your own address in the Mail To: box. This is handy when you're trying out the various options.

1 To compose a message, click the New message button, select New Message from the Mail menu or press Ctrl+N.

New Message

2 A Message window appears.

3 Enter the e-mail address(es) of the recipient(s). You can have several addresses on the To: and Cc: lines – separate them with semicolons.

4 Fill in the subject line.

If you have Microsoft Word or Excel, you can spell-check your messages. Select Check Spelling from the Mail menu or press F7.

5 Compose your message.

6 Click the Send [icon] button, select Send Message from the File menu or press Alt+S. This doesn't despatch the message, it simply places it in the Outbox.

7 To actually send the message, connect to the Internet, then click the Send and Receive button, select Send and Receive from the Mail menu or press Ctrl+M.

Send and Receive

...contd

Many Web pages have special links which enable you to send mail to their authors. For this to work, though, you need to have specified a default mail application.

1 Select Options from Internet Explorer's View menu and click on the Programs tab.

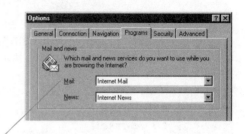

2 Check that Mail is set to Internet Mail.

The special links are generally in the form of an underlined name or e-mail address, a 'send mail' message or a picture of an envelope or postbox.

HANDY TIP

To find out more about the Planet Science Web site, turn to page 82.

1 If you hold the mouse pointer over one of these special links, you'll see an address beginning with mailto: in the Status bar.

REMEMBER

Don't forget to send your messages! It's very easy just to transfer them to the Outbox and then forget all about them.

2 Click on the link to send a message. The New Message window pops on to your screen, with the address already filled in. Follow the instructions on the previous page to complete and send the message.

Attachments

You can also mail pictures and document files to your friends and colleagues. This is handy if you're working from home or collaborating on a report.

Some e-mail packages don't support attached files, so if you're sending a message to someone who doesn't use Internet Mail, try to keep things simple.

1 Compose your message as usual (see page 131), then click the Attach File 📎 button. Alternatively, select File Attachment… from the Message window's Insert menu.

2 Locate the file you want to send and click Attach.

3 The file is added to the message, which can then be sent as normal.

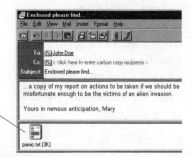

If you view the message in a separate window – see overleaf – you'll see the attachment as an icon. Double-clicking on it opens the attached file.

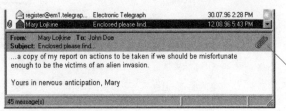

4 Paperclip icons alert your friend to the attached file.

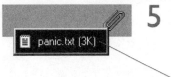

5 He or she then clicks on the gold paper clip to see the name of the attached file. Clicking on the file name opens the file in a suitable application, such as Notepad.

As long as the other person has the appropriate software for viewing it, you can attach pretty much any type of file, although attaching very large files may cause problems.

Receiving Mail

Unlike 'real' mail, e-mail messages aren't automatically delivered to your door – or in this case, computer. When someone sends you an e-mail, it's delivered to your service provider's mail server, which puts it into your personal mail box. You must then log on and collect it.

HANDY TIP

If you're having problems connecting to the Internet, select Options from the Mail menu and click on the Connection tab. Make sure the right type of connection is selected.

1 To check your mail, run the Mail applet and click Send and Receive. It should then prompt you to connect to the Internet (if necessary), send any messages which are waiting in your Outbox and fetch any new mail. The new messages are placed in your Inbox.

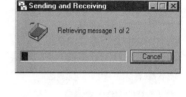

2 Click once on a message to display it in the Preview pane, or twice to display it in a separate window.

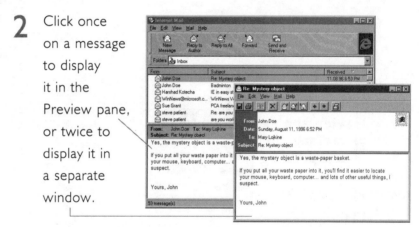

Replying and Forwarding

It's easy to reply to a mail message, because Internet Explorer automatically adds the correct address.

| To reply to a message, open it, then click the Reply to Author button (if you've opened the message in a separate window, use the button). Alternatively, select Reply to Author from the Mail menu or press Ctrl+R. Internet Explorer opens a New Message window.

HANDY TIP

If you don't want Internet Mail to quote the previous message, select Options from the Mail menu and click on the Send tab. Uncheck the Include message in reply box.

2 The To: and Subject: lines are already filled in, and the text from the previous message is quoted at the bottom.

3 Type your reply, then delete any superfluous material from the bottom section – leave just enough so that the recipient can see which comments you are responding to.

HANDY TIP

The Reply to All buttons and menu option enable you to respond to messages which have been sent to more than one person. Your reply will go to all the people who received the first message.

4 Click the Send  button.

Forwarding messages

You can also divert a mail message to a third party.

| To forward a message, open it and click the Forward button, select Forward from the Mail menu or press Ctrl+F. Enter the new address in the To: line.

2 Follow steps 3 and 4 above to add any comments you wish to make and send the message.

Organising Your Mail

Internet Explorer also enables you to sort your messages, delete the ones you won't want to refer to again and create folders to file the rest into.

HANDY TIP

The grey triangle ▽ **indicates which tab has been used to sort the folder. It points upwards for an ascending (A–Z, 1–10, etc) sort , and downwards for a descending sort. You can also change the categories by selecting Columns... from the View menu.**

1 To sort the messages in a folder, click one of the grey tabs at the top of the message list. Click again to reverse the sort.

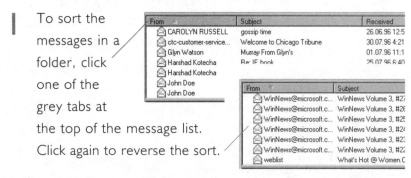

2 To delete a message, click once to select it. Select Delete from the File menu or press Ctrl+D or Delete to move the message to the Deleted Items folder. You can retrieve it if you change your mind – simply move it into another folder (see below). To delete a message permanently, open the Deleted Items folder and delete it again.

3 To create your own folders, pull down the File menu and hold the mouse over Folder. When the pop-up menu appears, select Create...

HANDY TIP

Your new folder is added to the Folder bar's drop-down list, enabling you to select the folder and read, sort or delete the messages you've filed into it.

4 Give your folder a name and click OK.

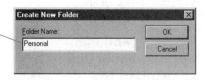

5 To move messages into your new folder, select them, then select Move to and choose a folder.

Address Book

As you might expect, the Address Book enables you to store all the e-mail addresses you use regularly. You can then add them to messages more easily.

1 To open the Address Book, pull down the File menu and select Address Book...

HANDY TIP

It's even easier to add the address of someone who has sent you an e-mail message. Open the message in a separate window, then select Add to Address Book, Sender from the File menu. Alternatively, right-click on the name in the From: line and select Add to Address Book from the pop-up menu. Either action opens a New Contact form with the person's name and address already filled in.

2 To add an address, click the New Contact button or select New Contact from the Address Book's File menu.

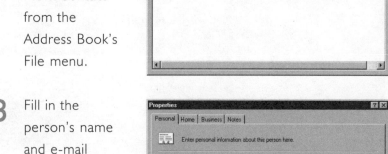

3 Fill in the person's name and e-mail address(es).

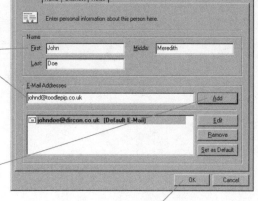

4 Click Add to add each of the person's e-mail addresses to the list.

5 Click the Home, Business and Notes tabs to add any other information you wish to keep track of.

6 Click OK to add the new contact to your Address Book.

...contd

Once you've added someone to your Address Book, you can send messages to them simply by selecting their name.

1 Create a New Message, then click on the index card icon at the beginning of the To: line.

2 Type the first few letters of the recipient's name.

3 Internet Mail jumps to the right part of the list.

4 Click the To -> or CC -> button to add the person to the recipient list. Select any further recipients, then click OK to return to the Message window. The recipient(s) will have been added to the To: and/or Cc: lines and you can complete the message.

Address Groups

If you often 'broadcast' messages to groups of people, you can create a mailing list by copying their details into one or more 'Address Groups'.

BEWARE

When you send a message to a Group, it is automatically sent to everyone on the list. Many people have embarrassed themselves by accidentally sending a private message to all the people in an Address Group.

1. To create a Group, open the Address Book and click the New Group button, or select New Group from the File menu.

New Group

2. Give the Group a name.

3. Click Add to select the members from your Address list.

4. Select a member, then click Add -> to copy them across. Repeat until the Group is complete.

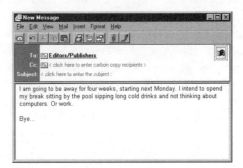

5. You can now send a message to all the people you selected, simply by addressing it to the Group.

Even if the people you know have nothing in common, an 'Everyone' group can be handy for notifying all your friends and colleagues of a change in address, forthcoming holiday or other special event.

Automatic Mail Checking

If you spend a lot of time on-line, or often receive urgent messages, you might want to instruct Internet Explorer to check your mail box at regular intervals.

1 Select Options from the Mail menu and click on the Read tab. Make sure the Check for new messages... box is selected and specify a time interval – perhaps ten minutes.

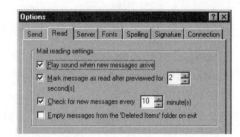

2 Internet Mail will then check for new mail – and send any messages in your Outbox – every ten minutes.

If you're off-line, Internet Mail attempts to connect you to the Internet. Depending on your setup, it will either dial your modem automatically or prompt you to connect. You can prevent this by closing Internet Mail when you log off.

If this doesn't work, select Options from the Mail menu, click on the Connection tab and try setting Connection: to I connect manually.

Alternatively, you may want to increase the time interval to, say, 60 minutes, and leave Internet Mail running. It will then check your mail, or prompt you to do so, at regular intervals. However, having your computer suddenly dial your modem can be quite disturbing, so you may prefer to do without automatic checking.

If you decide to let Internet Mail establish the connection automatically, make sure it's set to disconnect again once it has checked your mailbox.

Select Options from the Mail menu and click on the Connection tab. Make sure the Disconnect... box is checked.

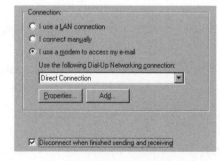

CHAPTER THIRTEEN

Newsgroups

Usenet newsgroups enable you to communicate with
Internet users who share your interests.

Covers

Newsgroups Explained

The Usenet newsgroups are the Internet equivalent of your local pub or social club. They're nowhere near as pretty as the Web, but they're a bit more interactive. If you're looking for gossip, trivia, advice, arguments and – very occasionally – news, Usenet is the place to find it.

Newsgroup 'messages' are also referred to as 'posts' and 'articles'. The three terms are interchangeable.

A newsgroup is essentially a public mail box dedicated to a particular topic. Anyone on the Internet can post a message, and anyone else can read it and upload a reply.

Unlike a Web page, though, the 'mail box' exists in more than one place. All the messages are regularly copied from one news server to another, enabling you to access them locally. Rather than connecting to lots of sites from all over the globe, you simply download the latest messages from your service provider's news server.

There are over 15,000 newsgroups to choose from. Some have a close-knit community of regular posters; others are larger and more anonymous. Either way, though, there's almost certain to be someone who wants to share your experiences, answer your questions, ask you for advice or just pass the time of day.

Understanding Newsgroup Names

Newsgroup addresses look like:
```
rec.arts.movies.reviews
```

or sometimes:
```
news:rec.arts.movies.reviews
```

Newsgroups are organised hierarchically: each section of the address (moving from left to right) reduces the scope of the group. In this case `rec` stands for recreation, `arts` and `movies` are self-evident and the group only carries `reviews`. There are ten other `movies` groups, about 100 other `arts` groups, and over 500 `rec` groups in total.

`rec` is only one of hundreds of top-level categories. Fortunately, you can find almost everything you want in just seven sections: `alt`, `comp`, `news`, `rec`, `sci`, `soc` and `uk`.

...contd

HANDY TIP

The `alt.` `binaries` **newsgroups contain messages with attached files – pictures, sounds, extra levels for games and so on. It's generally easier to get these files from Web or FTP sites, though.**

alt (alternative)

Almost anyone can create an `alt` newsgroup, so the `alt` hierarchy is one of the liveliest and busiest sections of Usenet. Some of the groups are pretty wild, but most are just odd – if you're interested in alien conspiracies, urban legends or breakfast cereal (no, really), `alt` has much to offer. It's also a nursery for new groups, some of which eventually graduate to the more respectable hierarchies.

Typical Group: alt.comedy.british
The `alt.comedy.british` newsgroup covers all forms of British comedy, including radio, written and live, but television dominates. Both classic and current series are discussed, generally with warmth and affection.

comp (computing)

The `comp` groups cover everything from hardware and software to artificial intelligence and home automation.

Typical Groups: comp.os.ms-windows hierarchy
The 51 `ms-windows` groups cover setting Windows up, software, utilities, networking and so on. Alternatively, try the 26 `comp.sys.ibm.pc` groups, which deal with demos, games, hardware and miscellaneous other topics.

news (Usenet)

The `news` groups cover Usenet itself, and are mostly unexciting. `news.announce.newusers` contains lots of information for beginners.

rec (recreation)

The `rec` groups covers hobbies, sports, arts and music, and are the best place to start. They tend to be friendlier than the `alt` groups and it's easy to find your way around.

Typical Group: rec.ponds
Like most of the specialist `rec` groups, `rec.ponds` is either a gold mine or a waste of space, depending on whether you're interested in the subject matter. Whatever your question, someone will have the answer – and be willing to share it with you.

sci (science)

The `sci` groups cover mathematics, physics, engineering, chemistry, biological science, medicine, psychology and philosophy – everything except computing, basically.

Typical Group: sci.space.shuttle
The `shuttle` newsgroup covers both the shuttle and the forthcoming international space station. It's peopled mostly by enthusiasts, rather than specialists, so it's more approachable than you might expect. It doesn't have the good looks or real-time features of NASA's Web site (see page 82), but you do get to discuss your ideas rather than just sitting and watching.

soc (social)

The `soc` groups deal with social issues. The biggest subsection, `soc.culture`, has well over 100 groups dedicated to various countries and cultures. Genealogy, history and religion are also well represented, and there are a number of support groups.

Typical Group: soc.couples
The `soc.couples` group covers heterosexual relationships (try `soc.motss` if you're interested in 'members of the same sex'). It tends to be dominated by Americans and is mostly concerned with the niceties of dating and the allocation of chores.

uk (United Kingdom)

The uk groups are a microcosm of Usenet as a whole. The most popular groups are `uk.politics` and `uk.misc`, but you'll also find job ads, an *Archers* group and a selection of `rec` and `religion` groups.

Typical Group: uk.politics
The members of `uk.politics` are no more likely to reach a consensus than a random selection of MPs, and they can be every bit as belligerent, so be prepared for some lengthy arguments. There are also several subgroups which cover major issues such as the constitution, crime, drugs and the environment.

Getting Started

You'll need to know the address of your service provider's news server to configure Internet News. You'll also need to know whether you have to enter a password when you connect to it.

If you can't run Internet News from Internet Explorer, it's probably because it hasn't been specified as your default news application. Follow the instructions on page 132, substituting 'News' for 'Mail'.

If you didn't get the Internet News applet with your copy of Internet Explorer, follow the instructions on page 129 to download and install it.

1 To run Internet News, select it from the Programs section of the Start menu, or select Read News from Internet Explorer's Go menu, or click on the Mail button and select Read News. The first time you do this, the configuration Wizard runs, enabling you to enter your account details.

2 You'll then be prompted to connect to the Internet so that the list of available newsgroups can be downloaded. This usually takes a few minutes.

3 The newsgroup list appears. You now need to select interesting newsgroups and 'subscribe' to them. It's a good idea to log off while you do this.

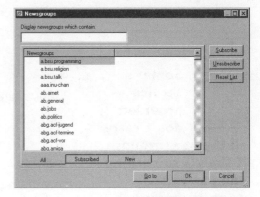

Subscribing to a newsgroup isn't like subscribing to a magazine or club – you don't have to pay anything, and it doesn't add you to a membership list. Subscribing simply tells Internet Explorer that you're interested in particular groups. It then displays those groups in the Newsgroups drop-down list.

...contd

HANDY TIP

If you're not sure where to start, try news.announce.newusers, news.newusers.questions, news.answers **or some of the groups listed on pages 143–4.**

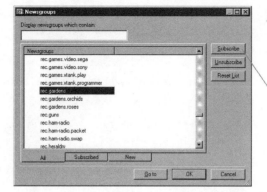

4 Scroll down the list until you find a group which looks interesting, select it and click the Subscribe button.

5 To find groups concentrating on a particular subject, try typing a word which the name might contain into the Display... box.

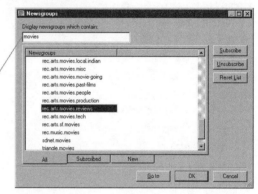

HANDY TIP

Some service providers don't carry all the newsgroups. If there's something you particularly want, try asking if it can be added to their list.

6 Click the Subscribed tab to see a list of the groups you have subscribed to. If you change your mind about a newsgroup, you can delete it from the list by selecting it and clicking Unsubscribe.

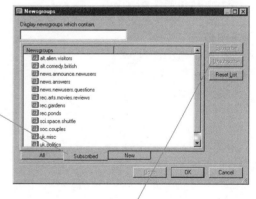

7 If you want to add to the list later on, click Newsgroups, select Newsgroups... from the News menu or press Ctrl+W.

Reading Messages

Some groups are very busy and receive hundreds of new messages each day. You can tell Internet Explorer how many headers to download at once by selecting Options... from the News menu. Click on the Read tab and enter a number in the Download headers... box.

Reading newsgroup messages is similar to reading mail (see Chapter Twelve).

1 Select one of your subscribed newsgroups from the drop-down list, then click the Connect button to connect to the Internet (if necessary).

2 Internet Explorer downloads the headers (titles) of all the new messages.

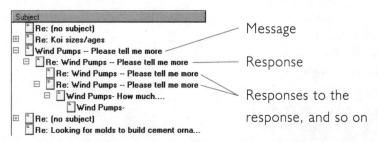

3 Click on a header to display the body of the message in the Preview pane, or double-click to display it in a separate window.

Threading

It can take a day or two for a newsgroup message to be copied to every news server. As a result, you'll sometimes see replies to a message before the original reaches your server.

Internet Explorer automatically 'threads' newsgroup messages – any message posted in response to a previous one is displayed immediately below the original.

Subject
- Re: (no subject) ———————————————— Message
- Re: Koi sizes/ages
- Wind Pumps -- Please tell me more
  - Re: Wind Pumps -- Please tell me more ——— Response
    - Re: Wind Pumps -- Please tell me more
      - Re: Wind Pumps -- Please tell me more
        - Wind Pumps- How much.... ————— Responses to the
          - Wind Pumps- ———————————— response, and so on
- Re: (no subject)
- Re: Looking for molds to build cement orna...

Click the ⊞ and ⊟ boxes to expand and condense the threads.

...contd

News messages don't stay on the server forever; your service provider keeps clearing them out to make way for new ones. If a group is very busy, they may only be accessible for a day or two, so check popular groups regularly.

Reading Messages Off-line

The main difference between reading mail and reading news is that downloading a newsgroup message is a two-step process. The header is downloaded when you select the group, but the body of the message isn't fetched until you click on its header. This means you don't waste time downloading messages you aren't interested in.

You can minimise the amount of time you spend on-line, and hence your phone bill, by 'marking' the messages which look interesting and downloading them all at once. You can then log off and read them.

1 Download the headers for one or more newsgroups (see previous page), then log off.

2 Mark the messages you want to download by clicking on them and selecting Mark Message for Download from the Offline menu. You can also mark complete threads, or even all the messages in a group.

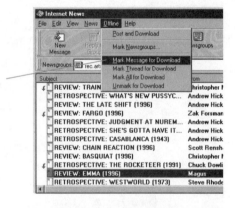

Marked messages have a green arrow ↲ to the left of the message icon. It is replaced by a pin 📌 when the message is downloaded.

3 Select Post and Download from the Offline menu. Internet News prompts you to reconnect, then downloads the marked messages.

4 Disconnect, read the messages and compose any responses or new messages (see opposite).

Posting Messages

You should read pages 150-2 before you start posting messages to newsgroups.

Posting messages is similar to sending mail, except that you address the message to the newsgroup.

1 To create a new message, select the group from the drop-down list, then click the New Message button, select New Message to Newsgroup from the News menu or press Ctrl+N.

If your response won't be of interest to anyone other than the original poster, you can e-mail it directly to them. Click Reply to Author, select Reply to Author from the News menu or press Ctrl+R to create a pre-addressed form.

2 To respond to an existing message, select it, then click Reply to Group, select Reply to Newsgroup from the News menu or press Ctrl+G.

3 Either way, Internet News brings up a pre-addressed New Message window. If you're responding to a previous message, the original text is quoted (see page 135).

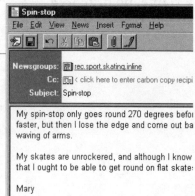

4 Compose your message, then click the Post button, select Post Message from the File menu or press Ctrl+S. This transfers the message to the Outbox.

5 Once you've composed all your messages, select Post and Download from the Offline menu to connect to the Internet and upload them.

Netiquette

Usenet has a reputation for being hostile to beginners or 'newbies'. While it's true that some groups are hard to break into, most welcome anyone who displays a little common sense and courtesy. In particular, try to adhere to the following guidelines, known collectively as 'netiquette'.

A 'flame' is an abusive message. Some groups tolerate and even encourage flaming; others expect members to be civil. If you post a flame, be prepared to get flamed back!

1   Always read the FAQ (see opposite) before you start posting messages, to avoid (a) posting messages that are inappropriate or (b) asking questions that have already been answered hundreds of times.

2   Don't post the same message to several groups at once. This is known as 'cross-posting', and it irritates the people who end up downloading your message several times.

3   Don't ever post the same message to lots and lots of newsgroups. This is 'spamming', and it irritates everyone. Sadly, you'll encounter lots of spam on Usenet, mostly in the form of ads for moneymaking schemes. Ignore them – responding just makes things worse.

4   If you're replying to a message, don't quote more of the original than is necessary – most people won't want to read it all again. It's helpful to quote the sentence or two you're actually responding to, though.

5   Don't type your message entirely in upper case. This is known as SHOUTING, AND IT MAKES YOUR MESSAGE DIFFICULT TO READ.

FAQs

A FAQ is a compilation of Frequently Asked Questions –
and their answers. FAQs exist for two reasons: to set out
the group's scope and rules, and to answer all the
questions a newcomer might ask.

**'Lurkers'
read the
messages
in a
newsgroup, but
don't post
anything. This is
how most people
start off – it's a
good way to get a
feel for what is and
isn't acceptable in a
particular group.**

Most FAQs are posted regularly, generally weekly or
monthly. If you 'lurk' in a newsgroup for a while, reading
all the messages but not posting anything, the FAQ should
eventually appear. You can also find FAQs for many
newsgroups at:
`http://www.cis.ohio-state.edu/hypertext/`
`faq/usenet/`

If all else fails, post a polite message asking someone to
point you in the right direction. Note that some groups
don't have FAQs; others have more than one, and some
FAQs serve several groups. If you can't find an appropriate
FAQ, lurk for a week or two to get a feel for the group.

Many FAQs represent the collective knowledge of all the
members of the newsgroup, and they can be fascinating
reading in their own right. The `rec.sport.skating.`
`inline` FAQ, for example, covers everything from buying
your first skates to skating backwards down flights of
stairs. If you're a coffee drinker, check out the Coffee and
Caffeine FAQ, which describes both the substance and the
drink in loving detail.

Smileys and Acronyms

Smileys and acronyms speed things up and enable you to clarify your comments.

Smileys

HANDY TIP

Smileys are also referred to as 'emoticons'. Don't use too many – some people think they're a bit silly.

It's difficult to convey emotion in a brief text message. This can lead to misunderstandings, particularly if you're prone to bluntness or sarcasm. As a result many people use 'smileys' – little faces made from keyboard characters – to convey their state of mind.

There are many, many smileys, but the two you're most likely to encounter are:

: -)	happy, or 'only joking'
: - (	sad or disappointed

(Turn the book through 90 degrees to see the faces.)

Acronyms

Common phrases are often abbreviated to just their initials, producing TLAs (Three-Letter Acronyms) and ETLAs (Extended TLAs). You'll also come across a few phonetic abbreviations.

Common acronyms and abbreviations include:

AFAIK	As far as I know
B4	Before
BTW	By the way
F2F	Face to face
FYI	For your information
<g>	Grin
IMHO	In my humble opinion
IMNSHO	In my not so humble opinion
ISTM	It seems to me
ISTR	I seem to recall
IRL	In real life (meaning, off the Internet)
L8R	Later
ROFL	Rolling on floor laughing
RSN	Real soon now
RTFM	Read the (guess) manual

Index